Mississippi
& After

A Life in Equal Justice Law

by Gil Venable

One Monkey Books
San Francisco

One Monkey Books
156 Diamond Street
San Francisco, CA 94114
415-431-8822
OneMonkeyBooks.com
Publisher@OneMonkeyBooks.com

ISBN 978-1-940722-04-7

Contents

Dedication

I met my wife Chris after many of the events in this book had happened. She has kindly consented to my telling old tales of love in a dangerous time.

Preface

This memoir by the late Gil Venable (Gilbert Tuckerman Venable, 1942-2019) may interest especially young and future attorneys who want to work for more equal rights and opportunities for all. Much of it is about the American Civil Liberties Union (ACLU) and the Lawyers' Committee for Civil Rights under Law (LCCRUL), both of which continue their good work today. The book may also appeal to progressive lay folk who want to reflect on their own family backgrounds, current lives and surroundings, and what changes they can help achieve. In his own, partially completed preface, Gil wrote the following.

"I was half boy, half man in the mid-'60s, a time of innocence and evil when ideas about love and equality were changing from winter to spring. My own feeling was that all people should have a fair chance to make something of themselves. This notion seemed to compel me to do stupid, but exciting, things. It was a time to sing the Mississippi blues or build a new Jerusalem. By luck, I was a witness stuck in the most exciting of it. By the end of a summer, I was hooked on the quest for equality (not only in the South) and was no longer afraid of death.

"To understand American equality, past and present, I have tried to see history through the eyes of a few ordinary people who were my forebears. I tell a few of their stories to help set my place in the bigger picture.

"In these pages I often use terms that were commonly accepted at the time. Before the late '60s (when James Brown belted out *Say it loud, I'm Black and I'm proud*) 'Negro' was the accepted and respectful term for Americans of African descent. White "moderates" in the South had difficulty with the pronunciation. Try as they might, it would come out 'Nigra,' as in, 'Our Nigras are *good* Nigras.' But my wise mentor lawyer Marian Wright Edelman would educate them: 'Knee,' she would begin by saying and touching her knee. Then she would lift her hand gracefully upward and say, 'Grow.'"

Gil completed a basic manuscript around 2009, then revised it over several years, deleting personal content to make it more appealing to potential academic publishers. We have reinstated some of his redactions to give a richer, more intimate picture of the life that inspired him and brought him joy. We have also added footnotes telling a bit more about some of the people he mentions and providing more background for readers less familiar with the American struggle for equal rights, north and south, from the 1940s onward. For a good, brief summary of the long-term role of legal support groups in shaping equal rights in Mississippi through and beyond the 60s, see Frank R. Parker's *Black Votes Count: Political Empowerment in Mississippi After 1965,* University of North Carolina Press, 1990. pp 79-82.

A dedicated and discerning lifelong listener to and collector of the music in the air, Gil explored all corners of classical, rock, pop, Motown, blues, folk, alternative, counter-culture, and other contemporary song. We've italicized some of the lyrics he embedded in his tale.

At his passing Gil hadn't yet listed acknowledgements. We're sure he would have wanted to thank more individuals than we can name here. We thank Mel Leventhal for extensive and frank feedback to Gil and to us. George Chaffey generously shared his own diaries, records, and recollections, which include glimpses of Gil. Kerry Gough shared his own experiences with us in person and through his own moving memoir, *Dear Jeff.* We also want to thank Melvyn Zarr, Henry Aronson and Calvin Lee. Special thanks also to Marian Wright Edelman for her support and several photos.

We've taken the liberty of using a few photos by professional photographers without permission. For most we tried to request permission but did not hear back. In appreciation of their work we have made donations to the ACLU and the Southern Poverty Law Center.

—Chris Locke & Alan Venable

Fairness, Justice
& the Stories of My Father

My father loved Guatemalan shirts, which likely reminded him of the Guatemalan refugees whom he assisted in the early 1980s. We were always introduced to new cultures not only through the usual food and festival children's experience, but by meeting different people directly. This has shaped my entire life, in that I am rarely afraid of difference. This is a value brought to me in part by my father.

I was able to observe, through many hikes with conservationists, the stunning beauty of nature. The story of the efforts of these conservationists, when successful, was inspiring. Places and people my father helped included keeping Fort McDowell Reservation from being flooded by Orme Dam and protecting the Grand Canyon from air tours.

He worked tirelessly for compensation for the Navajo uranium miners, though he did not win, because of a Cabinet Level decision to do research on people drinking uranium and exposed to it, without any knowledge. We do not always win. We try.

My father found common cause with people with disadvantages, once improved the monitoring system for the state of Arizona with regards to educational equity for persons with disabilities. This influenced my view of fairness and of equality.

Wendsler Nosie went to Mount Graham to pray as a part of his preparation for his daughter's upcoming sunrise ceremony. He was arrested for trespassing on the University of Arizona property (the observatory) which was still Apache sacred land. I learned that the law is not always absolute, because it needs to be negotiated.

I was lucky to see many tales of justice and fairness at the skilled hands of my father as supported by my mother. He gave me an example of what could be accomplished legally and strategically. I am happy to present to you my father's stories, which combine and merge with my stories of my father.

—Elizabeth Venable, MA, MPA

Gil Venable, 1964.

South

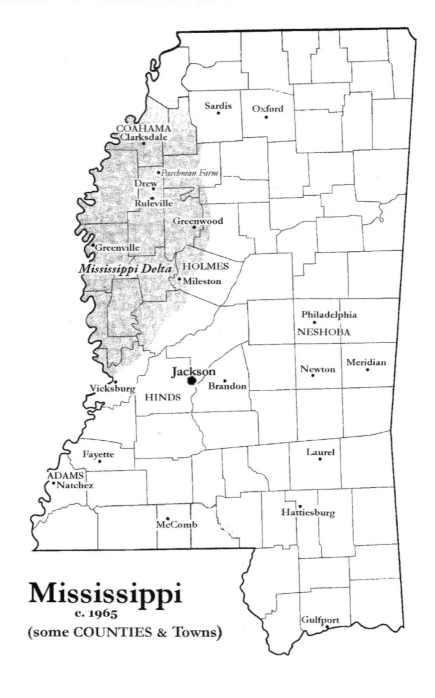

Sardis
Oxford

COAHAMA
Clarksdale

Parchman Farm

Drew

Ruleville

Greenwood

Greenville

Mississippi Delta   HOLMES
Mileston

Philadelphia
NESHOBA

Newton   Meridian

Jackson   Brandon

Vicksburg
HINDS

Fayette

Laurel

ADAMS
Natchez

Hattiesburg

McComb

Mississippi
c. 1965
(some COUNTIES & Towns)

Gulfport

1. *Road to Darkness*

I'd ridden my Honda 300 motorcycle from Pittsburgh to Briarcliff Manor, a small town up the Hudson where the Foldeses were kindly letting me park it for the summer behind their new suburban home. Jewish-Unitarian-Hungarian refugees from around 1940, they'd formerly lived in Pittsburgh where one of their three daughters had been part of LRY, our Unitarian church youth group. From Briarcliff, I hopped the Greyhound down to New York's Port Authority, arriving a little late. Still, coming out of the terminal I stopped to buy a hot NYC bagel before I went looking for the bug.

"I'm Gil," I said as I went around front to throw my battered suitcase in the trunk of the old VW beetle.

"We know," said the driver. "We've been waiting."

This was Bill Robinson, a Black law student at Columbia I'd met at an orientation conference in March. From a recruiting brochure there, I'd learned they needed "attorneys who will go south for three or four weeks (more if possible) who will work under uncomfortable, even hazardous conditions."

It promised poverty-level living in remote, poor Black communities. The legal work might be in front of justices of the peace or inside jails or sheriffs' offices. "There may not be a good law library in a hundred miles, nor a competent legal secretary, nor a law enforcement official or judge who will extend to you the minimal courtesies, to say nothing of due process." Although it went without saying that no pay was offered them beyond what the firms of those who worked for one might be willing to put up to sustain them, hundreds of lawyers were signing up.

Bill was treasurer of "Lizcrick", the newly formed Law Students' Civil Rights Research Council (LSCCRC) that I'd joined in order to work with the lawyers. The other two law-student passengers introduced themselves: riding shotgun was Mel Leventhal, a dark-haired NYU law student, always in motion; in back where I crawled in was Alice White from Yale.

We four northern students (three men, one woman, three white, one Black) were much alike and all of us eager to get down south to work as volunteers (not paid exactly, but with some expenses reimbursed). Lizcrick had links with the Lawyers' Constitutional Defense Commit-

1

tee (LCDC), which had organized the training in March and was also working on civil rights down there. Both groups had space in the American Civil Liberties Union (ACLU) offices in New York. Add to this spaghetti of acronyms the Lawyers' Committee for Civil Rights Under Law (LCCRUL), a fourth interwoven, northern-based group for which I'd soon be working in Jackson, Hinds County, Mississippi.

En route to Jackson we'd be dropping Alice off in Atlanta. It was June 9, 1965, before the interstate freeway system had grown to what it is today. Our drive would be mostly freeway south, then west on crowded business routes and country roads.

I had been a little late,[*] but was adept at shifting attention. "Hey, did you hear about the oral argument before the Supreme Court in the *Eros* case?" They knew what I was talking about—a suit involving some color nude photos of a Black man and white woman together that had been published in the erotic hardcover magazine *Eros* but banned as obscene.[†]

"Are those the same pictures that were up on the walls at that party?" asked Bill.

"Same photos," I said. "Our law librarian at Pitt (his wife is Black) had that issue squirreled away, but showed to students he could trust to be discreet."

Bill and I had met at the chic art gallery party, the closing event of the training where well-dressed intellectuals of all colors mingled but did not touch. In one room was (two decades before Colors of Benetton's first groundbreaking "United Colors" ads) a series of large, nude photographs of a very Black man and a very white woman. They were beautiful pictures, technically well done and, if you could get past the color barrier, no more provocative than, say, Rodin's sculpture "The Kiss." I wanted that sleek and soft white woman in the pictures for myself, yet at the same time I felt the Black man was my friend. Their embrace was gentle. They belonged together.

For me, staring at those photos was a powerful, life-changing moment. I had never seen anything like them. Abstractions became concrete and focused. They made me angry that in 1964 the Court of Appeals in *Ginzburg v. United States* (338 F.2d 12, 3rd Cir.) had banned such a beautiful thing.

---

[*] A lifelong tendency for Gil.

[†] Ralph Hattersley's color photo essay "Black & White in Color," published by Ralph Ginzburg in Issue 4, Winter 1962.

The case had now been argued again in the Supreme Court. Like a good law student, I summarized the law from the court's most recent pornography decision, *Jacobellis v. Ohio,* (378 US 184, 1964), saying something close to, "Justice Stewart was supposed to define the law so that people would know how to obey it, but all the turkey said was, 'I know it when I see it.' What are they going to try to do next? Erase those images from my brain?"

Silence.

Someone asked Bill what he thought about going out with white girls. He answered that he'd gone out with some darker skinned white girls, but wasn't particularly attracted to blondes.

Mel said something that to me suggested he'd had some experience with interracial dating, which I saw as the wave of the future. I was more puzzled by Bill's remark about the unattractiveness of blondes. It didn't jibe with my own physical attraction to them, nor with the southern stereotype that Black men lusted after blonde white women.

Bill said, "You better not be seen with your Black girlfriend in Mississippi, or pieces of your body will be found in the Tallahatchie River. All Emmett Till did was whistle." Bill had worked in the South the previous summer. It was part of his Lizcrick officer duties to clue us in to life down there.

Someone brought up the question of how "easy" different religions or races of girls might be.

Alice winced. "You guys are as bad as the professors who always call on women students when a case comes up involving sex."

The public schools I'd attended had been integrated for some time, and in school students generally got along well, ignoring racial and ethnic differences. I think this was partly because there were so many distinct ethnic groups (Anglo-Protestant or Catholic, Jewish, Black, Italian, Irish, Greek, Hungarian, Polish, Slovak, even here or there a Hispanic, Egyptian, or Asian.) Of course we all shared the Golden Rule. And, of course, many other students' parents set limits who could date whom.

When they asked what adventures I might have had already with Black girls, all I could say was no. There had been very few in my small mid-year-graduation classes from eighth grade and high school, and in the latter Black kids were often steered out of the "academic" track and into "industrial arts." The most I could say was how I had often talked with one scholarly girl in high school. I'd bumped into her back home after college. Her husband was working in the local civil rights movement.

A page from Ralph M. Hattersley Jr.'s beautiful photo essay in *EROS*, Issue 4, 1962, originally in color. *Gratefully borrowed.*

For me at the orientation in March, a second wake-up call had sounded as seasoned civil rights lawyers presented fascinating new courtroom strategies and solutions for the difficulties encountered in the southern courts the prior year during "Freedom Summer." Standing out from the rest of the speakers was non-lawyer James Farmer, talking passionately about the need to maintain nonviolent tactics in response to the violence of the Klan.

Having founded the Congress of Racial Equality (CORE) in 1942 (the year I was born) and its director in 1965, 45-year-old Jim had long and deep experience in the movement. He told us about the pine tree country of Northern Louisiana where CORE was using nonviolent techniques in organizing Black factory workers. In response, a 50-car Ku Klux Klan procession had driven through the Black community. In counter-response, local Black men, carrying their guns, met and started a movement called the Deacons for Defense.

School children were protesting outside a school. The police came to put the demonstration down. Four Deacons stepped out of a car and calmly loaded their shotguns. The police stepped back and the segregationist Governor of Louisiana stepped in to quell the violence by granting the Black demands. Farmer's dramatic telling of the story sold me. I was happy that I was going to Mississippi, where the actual beatings and killings were coming only from the white side. To me, it sounded like Mississippi might be safer for me than some other states.

It was Sunday as we passed through DC. The streets were nearly deserted.

Did Camelot ever exist? we wondered, seeing the white columns of the White House where the almost royal, young Kennedy family had seemed to be changing the nation.

None of us wanted to talk about the assassination, so the rhetorical question just hung in the air. Kennedy had proposed civil rights laws but had never made the effort needed to get them passed. That had become President Johnson's gift to the nation. In 1964 Johnson put tremendous energy into the passage of Kennedy's civil rights bill. He lobbied Congress tirelessly, calling personally on individual members of Congress to line up the necessary votes. He had a way of putting his huge, friendly arm around the shoulder of a senator or congressman, squeezing literally or politically, until he got agreement.

The civil rights act that became law on July 2, 1964 (42 USC § 2000) was the most important piece of civil rights legislation in the twentieth century.

5

In theory it opened all public accommodations, hotels, restaurants, swimming pools, to all Americans regardless of race, color, religion, or national origin. It provided for uniform voting tests and established a 6th grade education certificate as sufficient proof of literacy. The act also outlawed discrimination in employment on the basis of race or sex and established the Equal Employment Opportunity Commission to enforce that part of the law. One of our jobs in Mississippi would be to help in the long process of changing theory into reality.

In mid-March 1965, Johnson sent the final major civil rights bill of that time (the *Voting Rights Act of 1965* (42 USC § 1983) to Congress. On March 23 a successful Senate cloture vote of 77 to 19 ended a filibuster and signaled probable passage. As we drove south through Washington, we expected passage shortly.

I expressed some respect for Johnson's supporting it, after having been basically a racist all his life until now.

"You got that half right." said Bill. "He called us 'n-----s' and voted against a law that would have outlawed lynchings. I think he's like all politicians—no longer representing the southern state of Texas, but acting as President of the nation. Just doing what he feels will help him get reelected at a national level."

With a naïveté I immediately regretted, I speculated, "Maybe he had come to love and respect Kennedy, the man who selected him for the vice-presidency. He worked to get Kennedy's civil rights act passed because he was outraged at the assassination."

"Johnson's an enigma," said Alice. "Even back in the '50s he refused to sign the Southern Manifesto denouncing *Brown v. Board of Education* (347 US 483, 1954). There must have been some good in him then."

It was evening as we passed the Lincoln Memorial. A glow from behind seemed to bring the giant statue to life. I said he'd been our greatest president. Alice countered that although he'd done great things toward ending slavery he was still a racist at heart.

I was indignant at that last remark, but she pointed out how Lincoln had promoted the *Fugitive Slave Act*, which had sent runaway slaves who had made it to free soil in the North back to their masters in the South. She said emancipation had merely been his way of recruiting African Americans to fight for the Union. In any case, he'd started the Civil War to support the interests of the rich northern manufacturers over those of southern farmers, not to free the slaves.

I was stunned. In high school, American history had been all boring battles, dates and names, so I hadn't taken it in college. "You shouldn't belittle what he did in freeing the slaves," I objected. "In those days he can't have been expected to have thought much about corporate greed and social programs." Wanting to add some historic fact that would put Lincoln's positions into context I added, "Karl Marx didn't publish *The Communist Manifesto* until 1848."

"Hey, Venable," asked Bill, "what are you, a Democrat or a communist?"

I told him I'd been born a Republican. That stopped them all, briefly.*

Then someone countered by asking me whether being a Republican was a congenital disease rather than a choice.

"The way you talk, how can you be one?" Bill wanted to know.

"It's the party of Lincoln," I said.

"Didn't he die a while ago?" Bill asked. "Who did you vote for last year?"

That had been my first chance to vote. I had confessed to my mother (Regis Illston Venable, named after a nun and nurse her physician father had admired) that I was going to vote for Johnson rather than Goldwater. She said, "We're Republicans, but you should always vote for who you believe to be the best person, and you don't have to tell anyone who it is if you don't want to."

"That's a pretty private question," I told Bill, "but I voted for Johnson because he promised to get us out of the war in Vietnam."

It was many years later that, going through my parents' old papers, I found out why they'd been Republicans. During the Depression, having met at Cornell, both were active members of the Socialist Party. At university, my mother helped make and hand out leaflets. During or just after college, my father (Emerson Venable) became a socialist soap box orator. He was physically small, so he needed and had large "blockers" to protect him from hecklers as he spoke out against the evils of capitalism in the park. He was chased by the police in Binghamton, NY, while painting footsteps on the sidewalk leading to the rallying point where Norman Thomas, Socialist candidate for President, was to speak.

When my parents moved to Pittsburgh around 1935, the Socialist Party hadn't qualified to be on the ballot. The only registration choices were Republican or Democrat. They hated how the Demo-

---

* Gil did enjoy a tease.

crats had undermined and destroyed the Socialist Party, watering down its ideals in the so-called "New Deal." So they registered Republican.

We got to Atlanta as dawn was breaking, dropped Alice off and went to nap for the day in Julian Bond's apartment. In the Deep South in those days, cars with inhabitants of mixed races were often suspected

Emerson & Regis Illston Venable, 1990 (posed to make the gent look taller, of course.)

of being involved in civil rights and were pulled over by the local police.* Some riders had just been beaten, others ended up dead. To minimize those risks, we would follow the standard procedure of driving only at night for the rest of the trip.

Julian's apartment was equipped for work, not parties. Books were everywhere. Materials for his just-ending campaign for a seat in the Georgia House of Representatives were piled against the wall. Above them hung a "missing persons" poster with photos of Student Non-Violent Coordinating Committee (SNCC) workers Andrew Goodman, James Earl Chaney and Michael Henry Schwerner, although their bodies had been unearthed seven months earlier in Neshoba County, Mississippi.

A poster from SNCC showed a Black threesome, two men and a girl kneeling on a sidewalk in prayer, captioned, "Come let us build a new

---

* Southern highway patrols still stop integrated cars and grill the occupants about why they are traveling together. See Peter Jarrett-Schell's *Seeing My Skin (A Story of Wrestling with Whiteness)*, 2019.

world together." Another showed a Black hand reaching to the heavens, captioned simply, "NOW." In a jar on the kitchen table were SNCC pins with Black and white hands in a handshake. I asked if I could have one, and I have it still, although I have lent it to my elder daughter, Elizabeth.

Like me, Julian suffered from a boyish face, much younger than his twenty-five years. A few days later, along with ten other Black candidates, he won his seat, though the Georgia House would refuse to seat him because of his opposition to US policy of war in Vietnam. It would take a year until the United States Supreme Court ruled that the Georgia House had denied Bond his freedom of speech and was required to seat him.

Julian's pad had plenty of places to sit or work, but beds were in short supply, so several of us lay down on the floor, unable to sleep as SNCC veterans dropped in and out, treating us to some great stories. One of them, George Greene, told us about a march in Montgomery. On the march he'd been shot in the chest, but a Zippo lighter in his breast pocket had stopped a bullet and saved his life,

One of his friends had also been shot and was on the ground crying in pain, "My leg! My leg!"

George bent down to help and said, "Shit, man! That's blood dripping from your *arm*. Your leg's okay. Get up and start marching!" Which they did.

As we were leaving, I told him I liked his stories. He answered, "Your turn, white boy, I've been beaten in too many jails. I'm ready to leave the marching to others."

In fact, I would run into him again a few days later in the stockade jail in Jackson. He had been near the front in the freedom march, arrested, jailed, and beaten there again. He was bent over and I could see where police batons had darkened his olive shin.

I began to think his Zippo lighter story might be true. He was in pretty bad shape and asked for Maalox for his stomach. Outside, I got some from the Medical Committee for Human Rights (more about them in Chapter 3), labeled it with his name and followed the procedure to get it to him. A week later I learned that the jailors never delivered any medicine we sent in. I felt guilty for not having smuggled it in to him myself.

When it was dark, we left Atlanta and headed west across Alabama. Even in the darkness you could see the white cotton bolls in the fields and occasional run-down shacks. *I must be near Mattie's home*, I thought. I wondered whether she had ever picked cotton.

Mattie had to be better off in her small apartment in Pittsburgh—working in my family's 27-room mansion—than she would have been down here.

2. Iron City Roots

The big house where I'd been raised was in the nice East End, Shadyside neighborhood of Pittsburgh, on a stretch of Fifth Avenue once called "millionaire's row." It was a block from the former home of banker Richard King Mellon (torn down by then to make a park), and about four long blocks from the 19th century mansion-turned-art-museum of Henry Clay Frick, Andrew Carnegie's ruthless partner in steel. The place was now an art museum. Various other mansions of lesser historical significance still lined Fifth.

Our large but less notable home was built strong as a skyscraper on a steel frame. The massive exterior walls were made of large blocks of sandstone, trimmed with limestone. Being on a hill, it was four stories high in the back, three stories in the front. As children, we'd roller-skated on a tile-floored solarium, sometimes falling into the indoor fishpond. My mother hosted parties on the sprawling stone front porch. There were huge oak, maple, buckeye, and poplar trees and opulent rhododendrons. In the back yard, our father had filled in an artificial stream that had fed a pond lined with white coral. There were chandeliers and manteled gas fireplaces in many rooms. Eight bathrooms.

Those who looked closely could see that the old painted furniture in our home didn't quite live up to their surroundings. In plain pine dressers were the worn, hand-me-down clothes we boys wore. Our father's income as a chemist was modest, erratic in the 1950s, and never more than middle-middle-class, but the mansion and a full-time domestic gave an impression that allowed us boys to slip from one social class to another.

I was two in 1944 when we moved in. On that day, I went out in the large, overgrown back yard with my older brother, Wally. I wandered off into the trees and the lilac, hydrangea, wisteria, peony, and elderberry bushes and was eventually found in dismay, lost in my own back yard. But to us kids the yard and house never seemed like anything special.

Behind that modest front facade were 27 rooms.

Wally was a boy engineer, always building things like wooden "safes" or model planes. I had two younger brothers as well. Alan, two years behind me, gave his money to CARE while I spent mine on penny candy. To Tommy, the youngest, I taught math as I carried him on the crossbar of my bike to Liberty School. Except for the two years which separated our births, we four brothers looked like twins. Brown hair with cow licks sticking up from the back of our heads, brown eyes, pasty skin, and small mouths with monkey-like grins. We went to public schools and, thanks to our parents' all-in commitment to Scouting, were all early Eagle Scouts.

Before my parents bought it, the house had sat vacant for a handful of years. By then it was a real bargain, a fixer-upper at only $10,000. My father could repair the plumbing and refashion the kitchen around its turn-of-the-century, two-oven-plus-broiler, six-burner range. We could get tenants for the old attic-floor quarters. A big house matched his ego.

My mother's dream was a smaller home where housework would not dominate her life. One part of the deal between my parents was that my mother would have full-time cleaning help so she could spend time rearing us. So came Mattie Belle Herring, a high school graduate recently moved north and recently married Leo Herring, a plasterer, both from Alabama. In effect she became part of our family, like a second mother to me, staying through our parents' deaths fifty years later. Mattie was small, but strong enough to carry us around. When my parents entertained large numbers of guests, she'd wear a uniform.

Mama's boy at the Washington Monument.

Cowboy Gil & Mattie Belle Herring.

One night, most likely in the late 1950s, Daddy took me along when he drove Mattie home. It was past the hour when the street cars ran and past the hour when my mother thought it safe for her to walk home. As we drove down working-class Larimer Avenue, an Italian-looking group of young men seemed to glare at us from the shadow of Our Lady Help of Christians Catholic Church. A few blocks further, the glare was from Blacks. We climbed up Mattie's cracked cement steps into a house with so much mortar missing from the bricks that I worried it might fall down. Only this one time did I get to see the two rooms that she and Leo rented. They were neat, tidy and warm, but some things seemed amiss. The teapot from which Mattie offered us tea was broken and carefully mended, not like my mama's small everyday teapot which was shaped like a thatched cottage with roses climbing up the walls. I was glad that Mattie got to spend a lot of her time at our house.

To my night companions on the road to Jackson, I didn't know what to say about Mattie or the mansion, so I didn't mention either. Many years later I asked her what she had felt when Alan and I went South (she'd borne no children of her own). She answered that she was proud of us but terrified, not expecting we would return alive. I asked her if she had talked about that with my mother. She said that she and "Mrs. Venable" never really talked.

One day, when I was little, Mattie's husband Leo came to plaster some ceilings. Not only was he Black, he was huge. I was very much afraid of him. But I soon learned from Mattie that Leo, a former high school football star, was really a gentle giant.

Mel slept as we crossed the border into Mississippi.

Bill asked me, "Why did you decide to come?"

"Because I believe in freedom."

"Oh don't give me that crap," he said. "What really made you come?"

"My little brother, Alan, and Lisa were coming. I couldn't stay at home." I said.[*]

"Who's Lisa?"

"Just a girl," I lied.

Lisa Marshall. My mind drifted back about eight years to the fall of 1957 when I was a sophomore in high school. I was walking with her at night along an oak-lined residential street.

"How was the meeting with the mayor?" I'd asked.

"He's an asshole." This from the lips of a '50s grade-school girl, beautiful with rounded face, high cheekbones, framed by an uncontrolled mass of brown hair.

"I thought you Quakers believed everyone was good." I said.

"He may have that of God within him, but I couldn't see it," she replied.

We had been attending a youth seminar sponsored by the American Friends Service Committee in Pittsburgh called "Human Values in Urban Redevelopment." It was my first exposure to the politics of race. We were trying to find out about the African-American families that were being evicted from the Lower Hill District of Pittsburgh to make way for a domed arena. But I'd missed the first day of the seminar because it was a school day.

Lisa ran ahead of me, giving a glimpse of her slender legs. She was three years younger than I, although she didn't talk or look like it. She turned around.

---

[*] However, in his first term at Pitt Gil had already been studying cases related to civil rights, race and jury selection.

"Why didn't you come on Friday?" It sounded more like an accusation than a question.

"My parents wouldn't let me. My mother thinks that one day of high school is more important than real lives."

Lisa softened. "Yeah, I know. My mom made me get all my assignments and finish them before I could come."

"I didn't know you had much homework in grade school."

"Maybe in *your* day," she said.

"So, what did Mayor Lawrence say?"

"Nothing, but he talked a lot."

In bits and pieces she told me that our perennial Democratic Mayor (whom my parents detested) thought the area was blighted and the best way to get rid of the pimps, hookers and lowlife Negroes was to flatten the Lower Hill like Hiroshima and make everyone move into other overcrowded Negro neighborhoods. The mayor said all homeowners would be fairly paid for their loss. He meant the slumlords would be paid off, but the families and children living in those old brick row houses would get no help.

"He really said that?" I asked.

"No, but I could tell what he was thinking from the way he dodged every question we asked." Her face glowed with anger. I was glad she was pissed off at the mayor, not me.

"Look at those stars," she said to change the subject.

It was a magical, cold night.

"You don't see stars like that very often in Pittsburgh." I agreed.

I wanted to hold her hand as we walked back to the Quaker meeting house, but I knew she was too young. I didn't mind waiting.

"There's one thing I would like you to remember." I said.

"What's that?" she asked, looking up at me.

"Wherever you are, no matter how far away from me, those same stars will be looking down on us."

"Police ahead," Bill Robinson said calmly. I slid my white face down below the window—no seat belts in those days. The patrol car was stopped; we passed without incident.

Like my parents and my older brother Wally before me, I'd decided to go to Cornell after finishing high school in 1960, majoring in chemistry.

Wally was still there when I matriculated. He lived in a residence called Watermargin that had been founded by World War II veterans who had shared a desire to promote understanding between races and religions. All male then, it was pretty much like a fraternity, but they sang folk songs and discriminated less. Membership was by majority vote. To my mind, these guys lacked expertise in throwing parties, but I hung out there a fair amount.

Watermargin sponsored a debate between Malcolm X and James Farmer. It wasn't the strident argument about violence and non-violence that I'd expected. Malcolm was a tall, handsome man who looked like pain was coming from somewhere deep inside. I wondered if it might have something to do with his six years in the Massachusetts State Prison. I couldn't argue with his message that a man who truly loves freedom will do anything necessary to get it.

I couldn't decide who won, though Jim Farmer had the better smile, a wry grin that could express skepticism and love at the same time. His call to action seemed not much different from what I heard from Malcolm. He was committed to fighting back, but using new, nonviolent weapons. Malcolm X and Farmer differed on ideas but seemed to respect each other as people. Like Malcolm, Jim Farmer had spent time in jail, but as a leader of nonviolent protests. In 1961, he'd led the first "Freedom Ride" to desegregate southern interstate buses. Deboarding in Jackson, he'd been arrested and jailed for forty days.

By 1964, as I stood by watching, Cornell students were following his leadership, signing up for training in nonviolent resistance and heading south for "Freedom Summer."

For other diversion at college, I bought a used tuxedo so I could usher at concerts and get in free. Great orchestras came from Boston and New York, but I particularly remember Nina Simone and Odetta. Nina Simone sang "Strange Fruit," about the lynching of Black men, to me probably the most powerful song ever written. Then she swung into "Mississippi Goddam," a call to action.

They were great songs, but my mind was still wandering in Ivy League halls, far from the reality of Mississippi. On graduating in 1964, just about all I knew was that I did not want to be a chemist. I decided on law school without really knowing why and enrolled at Pitt, my live-at-home option.

In the spring of 1965, the Unitarian Rev. James Reeb had answered Martin Luther King's call to white ministers to march in Selma and was murdered on arrival. I attended the memorial service on campus. Although Pitt was famous for student apathy, there was a huge crowd, more than could fit into Heinz Chapel. That night busses carried 130 students down to Selma. I learned about them only after they'd left, but still I felt guilty for not being aboard. Shortly after that, toward the end of my first year of law, I applied to Lizcrick for the summer.

As I was leaving for Mississippi in June, my younger brother Alan was going down from Harvard to volunteer with SCOPE, the 1965 summer voter registration project of King's Southern Christian Leadership Conference. The previous summer he'd been a counselor at a camp in Vermont, run by Pete Seeger's older brother John. At the camp were a brother and sister, Michael and Amy Goodman. Andrew Goodman was their cousin, and most of the summer had been overshadowed by his June disappearance in Mississippi.

One place Alan worked for SCOPE was rural Calhoun County, South Carolina. I was glad I didn't know until after he got home that the Ku Klux Klan had sent a shotgun blast through his SCOPE house window there when he was out, and that he had been jailed for trespass for a sit-in at the courthouse in neighboring Orangeburg County.

I expected my parents to resist my Mississippi plan and the prospect of having two sons doing civil rights work in the South. To my surprise, they were supportive. My mother felt that she would have gone too, if she hadn't had so many responsibilities at home. My father gave me a paper written by my great grandfather William Henry "Hal" Venable (teacher, poet, and historical writer) about his own experience as a young man, traveling the South to learn about slavery firsthand.[*]

One of his many adventures took place at an inn or small hotel in Mississippi, where he met and befriended a waiter named Paul, a slave who was also a talented dancer, musician and storyteller. Paul had been a field hand and had been happily married on a plantation in the southern part of the state. Then his master had raped Paul's wife. In retaliation, Paul had attempted to kill the master, but shot him in the leg. For this offense Paul was sentenced to death; but the master valued him enough as a commodity to sell him instead to the keeper of the inn where Hal was staying. Paul's wife and her father were sold off to a sugar plantation.

---

[*] "Down south before the war. Record of a ramble to New Orleans in 1858." *Ohio Archaeological and Historical Quarterly*, Volume 2. No. 4, March 1889, pp. 488-513.

While Hal was staying at the inn, a number of slaves had mysteriously disappeared from nearby cotton plantations and apparently escaped north. Suspicion focused on Paul, and the garret of the inn was searched. A few slaves were found hidden there, including his father-in-law.

Paul was taken to a shed where he was bucked (bound too tightly to move) and beaten naked with rawhide to extract a confession. Paul said nothing. At this point, as a northerner and friend of Paul's, Hal was no longer safe at the inn, so he left for the slave markets of New Orleans.

After the Civil War, Hal published his notes and traveled southern Ohio lecturing about slavery. He also moved on to teacher training and to writing many published books of poetry, memoir, history, and fiction. But what great-grandfather had done was nothing to me. I was inventing for myself. And going down wasn't only my decision, it was a movement. It was America in motion, as America is always in motion.

Some of us who were headed to Mississippi liked to think of ourselves as the elite among civil rights workers. No one seemed to disagree. I didn't know it then, but seventeen individuals had been murdered there in civil-rights-related cases in the ten years before I went. I had heard only of the most famous ones (Medgar Evers, Emmett Till, Chaney, Goodman and Schwerner), and those deaths seemed irrelevant to my own safety. Like most young people, I considered myself immortal.

By the way, although a memoir of events fifty years past might rest on shaky grounds, I do still have a good memory for much of what I'm writing here, and it matches well the many details recorded in my surviving legal work product and other writings from that time, most importantly the long, almost daily letters I wrote to Lisa and my parents.

3. *Welcome to Mississippi*

I managed to get some sleep as Bill drove west on US 80 across the middle of Mississippi. On the morning of June 11 in Jackson (the state capital, population about 150,000), we drove directly to the main Black business part of town.

Just about all the civil rights groups had offices on Farish Street. Bill dropped me off at 233 North Farish, my base that summer in the office of the LCCRUL (Lawyers' Committee for Civil Rights Under Law), or the "Lawyers' Committee" as I may call it from here on. The Committee had been founded by Harrison Tweed and Bernard G. Segal, two past presidents of the American Bar Association.

The ABA was not an activist organization, and generally its leaders came from large corporate law firms; but despite not being quite the perfect fit at the start, it was certainly good to have this power base of the national legal community joining in to work on the advancement of the civil rights movement.

I was welcomed by John Honnold, a wise, droll, white-haired law professor from Penn, who then headed the storefront office.[*]

The outside was newly fronted with brick as protection from bombs. The inside was all remodeled, modern, air-conditioned, and staffed with legal secretaries, some of whom[†] came down from large northern law firms for a month, among them Mrs. Borden, a white, self-described "Jewish mama."[‡]

Others I recall were Pearl and Wilma, two Black women who had been hired nearby.[*] As we soon discovered, we were also much better

---

[*] Along with Gil, Cal law student George Chaffey was also assigned to the office. Having driven from Berkeley he was one of the few in Lizcrick with a car. After Peace Corps service, George joined a California county legal services staff and initiated a community immersion program that hired lawyers to live in and become real community members in selected parts of the county so that they would "live and think locally...and be able to work for changes in and with the community, not just in court or in the office."

[†] Probably all of the actual qualified *legal* secretaries. There were few if any in-state Black legal secretaries.

[‡] George Chaffey mentions Kitty Goldstein as another legal secretary volunteer from the north. In an end-of-summer report, one young Lawyers' Committee attorney, Richard Abel, mentions the office also had a stove, refrigerator and shower. In material ways he felt LCCRUL was ostentatiously wasting money, alienating the groups it meant to serve and partner with, which survived on next to nothing.

equipped with a legal library than any group on the street, and other civil rights legal groups in Jackson would also soon depend on it.

Our presence aside, Farish Street was already a hotbed of civil rights activity. The NAACP Legal Defense and Educational Fund, Inc., known as the "Inc. Fund," focused on school desegregation. The LCDC (Lawyer's Constitutional Defense Committee) was there as an arm for the ACLU (American Civil Liberties Union) and a coalition of other organizations. All these legal groups worked together on what needed to be done.

Other civil rights groups, as well, had offices on Farish. One was the umbrella group COFO[†] (Council of Federated Organizations) embracing SNCC, CORE and other groups that had taken part in the 1964 Mississippi Freedom Summer. Another was the MFDP (Mississippi Freedom Democratic Party), which had attempted to seat an integrated delegation at the 1964 Democratic Convention.

Yet another was MCHR (Medical Committee for Human Rights), a volunteer group of doctors, nurses and health science students who provided first-aid and other medical services for civil rights workers and demonstrators. MCHR also often sent health workers to demonstrations to be arrested so that they could render emergency care in the jails.[‡] Rallies were held at Farish Street's Morning Star Baptist Church and at the Shriners Temple. All of these were within a few blocks on Farish, along with many Black businesses.

Stanley ("Stan") M. Walker was an African American law student at Yale and a graduate of Harvard was also assigned to work with the Lawyers' Committee. He was the first of several law students with whom I'd share a place in Jackson. We set off together to find an apartment. The urban neighborhood around Farish was pretty much owned or managed by Blacks, so there was a feeling of safety and welcome. Nearby we located a small, affordable apartment. Since the rooms were totally empty, I bought a sleeping bag and an army cot at

---

[*] Apparently not *legal* secretaries. Rick Abel lamented the lack of local Black legal secretaries, noting, "The absence of Negroes in the office is very noticeable to our clients, particularly the presence of a white rather than a Negro at the reception desk."

[†] Mel Leventhal recalls this office being on John R. Lynch Street.

[‡] Some, like Phyllis Cunningham, got swept up willy-nilly. See John Dittmer's *The Good Doctors: The Medical Committee for Human Rights and the Struggle for Social Justice in Health Care*. Bloomsbury, 2009.

an army-navy surplus store. Stan's girlfriend would be down in a couple weeks, so he got the only bedroom. We picked up staples at a Black grocery store: cornflakes, Wonderbread, peanut butter, grape jam, a large package of baloney and a gallon of milk.

We walked swiftly back down to the office. Although it was still morning, the heat and humidity were oppressive. By the time we got there, I was drenched in sweat. It was not so much the intense sun that was getting to me, as the feeling that I was walking in an aquarium. Actually, the brilliance of the sun seemed wonderful after years of grey skies in Pittsburgh.

Professor Honnold looked crisp and cool in a light blue seersucker suit.

"How do you stand the humidity?" I asked.

"Slow down," he said. "Originally I was inclined to believe that the southern drawl and slow movement of white people down here might be genetic. But now I think the snail's pace is caused by the humidity."

The Lawyers' Committee had been in Mississippi since the previous summer, but with no staffed office. Back then it had been cautious about representing people who had been arrested at demonstrations. To avoid representing those who might have been intentionally breaking the law, it had limited itself to representing only ministers from the National Council of Churches.

The problem was that the ministers declined to accept the free representation unless those arrested with them were also represented. By the summer of '65, however, it was unrestricted in defending civil rights demonstrators. Still, being brand new on Farish Street, we had to work a little harder than the other civil rights law offices at convincing Mississippi grassroots leaders of our competence and dedication.[*]

Because the late President Kennedy had requested its creation, the Lawyers' Committee could also justly call itself the "President's Committee" when it needed to invoke prestige. To help me gain

---

[*] The Lawyers' Committee "Report on the Committee Office in the South June 2-August 6" claims its relations with the NAACP, MFDP and other movement groups were satisfactory overall. From Rick Abel's perspective they were "terrible." He reported that most grassroots civil rights workers needing help "would prefer a lawyer from LCDC or the [NAACP]," because (among other reasons) those lawyers were more in sync in style and more actively, daily sought out individuals and groups in possible need of legal help. Another weakness of the committee's approach was that, however sharp the lawyers they rotated in and out, many or most of the lawyers' stays were only several weeks.

access to libraries, courts and jails, Professor Honnold gave me a letter of introduction that spelled out this connection and mentioned our having been welcomed by the Mississippi Bar Association. To me, that welcome came across as an excuse for the state's own resident white lawyers to not take the cases of civil rights workers.* (Later that summer I would meet three local Black lawyers (Carsie Hall, Jess Brown and Jack Young) who risked their careers and more for the cause.)†

Professor Honnold was turning over the day-to-day office leadership to an outstanding young white New York attorney, John H. Doyle, III. The Lawyers' Committee seemed to have a little better budget than the other legal groups. We couldn't trust the police because by this time we were well aware that local Mississippi law enforcement had been involved in the murders of Chaney, Goodman and Schwerner. As we also knew, in Natchez the Klan had a new, radio-equipped car, bright red, prominently marked KKK (See Chapter 10). So we rented the fastest cars available to be able to outrun the police or Ku Klux Klan if necessary.‡ (As a further precaution, our own cars from out of state were re-registered with Mississippi plates.)

My Honda ride from Pittsburgh to Briarcliff Manor had included a detour up to Bennington College in Vermont to visit Lisa Marshall. No longer a child, she was still a beautiful enigma.

---

* Rick Abel says the Lawyers' Committee's attended regular lunch meetings with the Hinds County Bar Association and occasionally partnered with local lawyers. At the end of the summer Abel saw this contact as largely useless, though a few times the committee had benefited by the collaboration of white Mississippi lawyers. The most striking was in dealing with an out-of-control ("crazy, mentally unstable," according to George Chaffey, my law student office mate) Coahama County Attorney Thomas H. "Babe" Pearson, who had suddenly summoned about a hundred Black women under a generally disregarded state law by which they would be fined or incarcerated for the crime of having borne a second illegitimate child. "Please make arrangements for the care of your children...," Pearson wrote considerately in his letter informing them of their trial.

† Hall, Brown and Young had been active in cases since 1961, assisted by the NAACP. Apart from Marian Wright Edelman, who was admitted to the Mississippi bar around this time, Rick Abel thinks they were the *only* Black lawyers in the state bar in 1965 and the only other lawyers who would take civil rights cases.

‡ "Nonsense!" says Mel Leventhal. "Under no circumstances would we be allowed to outrun police."

Lisa, too, had decided to come to Mississippi, but had no job lined up. In Jackson I asked around and found an opening for her in the newly created Head Start program run by the Child Development Group of Mississippi (CDGM) based in Jackson. By coincidence another Pittsburgh acquaintance of mine, Howie Croft, was also working for it. Back home, he had established a tutoring program for Black youth in Pittsburgh's North Side, through which I had tutored one bright youth in math.

CDGM had roots in the Delta Ministry, a project of the National Council of Churches—the major ecumenical movement for Christianity in the United States, supported by about twenty Protestant and Catholic denominations. It provided food and clothing in the poorest areas of Mississippi and worked to bring health care and other governmental services to the Delta. The Delta Ministry also engaged actively in the civil rights movement. The Lawyers' Committee had been called to help steer them in their, so far unsuccessful, efforts to integrate the local courthouse.

Far more than a child care program, CDGM focused on the poorest Black families and worked for human rights, health care, education, opportunity, jobs, and adequate wages for everyone. It was constrained by governmental rules and funding, but these came from Sargent Shriver, the head of President Johnson's antipoverty programs, rather than the local white power structure.

Rather than taking a job in Jackson, Lisa decided to work for CDGM in a remote rural Delta community, Mileston in Holmes County, where her only available telephone was the pay phone in a community center created the year before by out-of-staters Henry and Sue Lorenzi (later Sojourner) to support local civil rights efforts. I was unlikely to see much of her that summer, so our friendship would need to continue by mail.

I didn't know what to expect when I walked into the Unitarian Church in Jackson the Sunday after I arrived. I had been told that without exception the white community in Mississippi was hostile to the civil rights movement. The advice to me before leaving the North was: "Most whites will consider you an outside agitator, a traitor, and a Communist."

I also knew that there were still segregated Unitarian-Universalist congregations in the deep South, but over the last ten years Rev. Ed Cahill, our current minister in Pittsburgh, had led the integration of churches in Charlotte, NC, and Atlanta. Anyway, I counted on the fact that Unitarians are not usually prone to violence.

23

I knew I was safe when I met a future Black Unitarian-Universalist minister, 34-year-old John Frazier, who was a member of the church and also sat on the National Board of the NAACP. I received a warm reception. Members even lent me a kitchen table and chairs for the very bare, tiny apartment I was then sharing with Mel.*

Two years earlier, led by white Rev. Donald Thompson, the church had voted to open its membership to all people. Only one person voted against the motion, but several families felt they could not stand the community pressure and left. Two Blacks joined.

Already in 1965, Donald and an old time church member had started a Head Start program, the first integrated preschool in Mississippi. He was a member of the Mississippi Human Relations Commission, a private organization trying unsuccessfully to get governmental cooperation. As far as I could learn, the Unitarian Church was the only group of local white citizens in Jackson who supported and practiced integration. Rev. Thompson served the Unitarian church in Jackson from 1963 until August 1965.

About a week after I left Mississippi he had just accompanied John Frazier somewhere and was going home to his wife Leila when a white man (almost certainly a member of the Klan) stuck a shotgun out of a light green sedan and opened fire. The first shot missed, but a second from him or someone else blasted Thompson in the back. It didn't kill him but badly injured his shoulder and a lung; some pellets had stopped just short of his heart. A big man, he joked from his hospital bed that the doctors said his weight would kill him, but it was his fat that had saved his life.

As he recovered, he ignored new threats from the Klan, saying, "I realize that the same nightriders may be out to finish the job, but why have a successor who would also be a target?" However, a few months later, after the FBI confirmed that the Klan had set a new hour for his

---

* Rev. Frazier's activism had begun in high school in Greenville, 1954, with wearing an armband in support of *Brown v. Board of Education*. Expelled for insisting that his high school principal also celebrate the decision, he undertook several one-man demonstrations, was arrested several times, became the second Black to apply for the University of Southern Mississippi, and went to Jackson to work with (continued) Medgar Evers. There he met Buford Posey, a Unitarian-Universalist alum of USM (and first white Mississippian member of the NAACP) who signed his college application. Around the time Gil met him, John Frazier left the state to avoid revenge by the Klan for talking openly with the FBI about the Chaney-Goodman-Schwerner murders of the year before. Outside Mississippi he moved on to activist ministry and the Black Power movement. (From sources including *mit.edu/people/fuller/unitarian*.)

execution, he accepted the advice of local friends and, a few hours before it, left the state.

About forty churches were burned by the Klan in Mississippi that year. It seemed a miracle that the Unitarian structure survived.

THOMAS H. PEARSON
COUNTY PROSECUTING ATTORNEY
POSTOFFICE BOX 913
CLARKSDALE, MISSISSIPPI

JULY 16, 1965

FLORENCE JOHNSON
339 ISSAQUENA
CLARKSDALE, MISSISSIPPI

FLORENCE:

    INFORMATION HAS BEEN RECEIVED BY THIS OFFICE INDICATING THAT YOU HAVE GIVEN BIRTH TO AN ILLEGITIMATE CHILD. I WOULD LIKE FOR YOU TO COME TO MY OFFICE SO THAT WE CAN DISCUSS THIS MATTER.

YOURS TRULY,

Pearson

THOMAS H. PEARSON
COUNTY PROSECUTING ATTORNEY

THP/PWP

THOMAS H. PEARSON
COUNTY PROSECUTING ATTORNEY
POSTOFFICE BOX 913
CLARKSDALE, MISSISSIPPI

JULY 19, 1965

VERGIA MAE SMITH
316 COMMERCE
CLARKSDALE, MISSISSIPPI

VERGIA MAE:

    PLEASE MAKE ARRANGEMENTS FOR THE CARE OF YOUR CHILDREN SO THAT YOU CAN REPORT FOR TRIAL ON THE CHARGE OF HAVING AN ILLEGITIMATE CHILD ON MONDAY, AUGUST 2, 1965. I WILL RECOMMEND TO THE COURT THAT YOU BE SENTENCED TO SERVE THIRTY DAYS IN THE COUNTY JAIL, BUT THE COURT HAS THE POWER TO SENTENCE YOU UP TO 90 DAYS IN JAIL OR A $250.00 FINE.

    I WILL EXPECT TO SEE YOU IN MY OFFICE ON THAT MORNING.

YOURS TRULY,

Pearson

THOMAS H. PEARSON

THP/PWP

4. Eight Hundred Jailed

About a dozen of us law students were beginning our work in Mississippi that summer. Compared to local civil rights workers who had been on the front lines, some for years, most of us were taking a significantly lesser risk. Then, too, at the end of the summer, we would head back to our northern schools and homes.

On June 14, three days after I arrived, hundreds joined in a prepared and peaceful march in Jackson, focused on the right to vote. The other side was also prepared, including "Thompson's tank," an armored vehicle purchase a few years before.

"We've got a larger than usual police force," Jackson Mayor Allen Thompson added. "It's twice as big as any city our size. We're going to be ready for them. They won't have a chance."

Mississippi laws deliberately prevented Blacks from voting. For example, of anyone attempting to register, the registrar could opt to require a "satisfactory" explanation of any paragraph of the Mississippi Constitution. Expert in making things hard for Blacks and easy for whites, local officials could also require complex procedures for proving "good character." As of 1963, in all of Mississippi only 1,636 Negroes (less than 1% of the Black population) were registered to vote. But *The Voting Rights Act of 1965* was poised for adoption in the US Congress, and everyone expected it to increase that number. Governor Paul B. Johnson, Jr., had called a special session of the Mississippi Legislature, asking them to approve a state constitutional amendment that would weaken enforcement of the coming federal act. The June 14 march was in protest.

I stood in the sweltering sun and watched from across the street as the marchers walked quietly, two abreast, along the sidewalks toward the state capitol grounds. Many were Black residents of Jackson, but others came from the Delta and other outlying parts. They were joined by whites from the North, who tended to be college-age men and women or ministers. Despite my hopes that first day, no one made it to the High Street grounds. About 400 men, women and children were arrested for "parading without a permit," which only encouraged others to march the next day. By the fourth day of marches, about 800 had been arrested and transported in sanitary department (garbage) trucks or trailers to makeshift stockades.

With only a year of law school behind me, these arrests put me to work with some of the best legal minds in America, starting with John Doyle and including Tony Amsterdam, Marian Wright Edelman, Henry Aronson (see Chapter 9), Christine Clark (Chapter 9), Melvyn Zarr (see below), James Starrs (Chapter 4), R. Kent Greenawalt, Alan Levine, Alvin J. Bronstein, and the legendary Bill Kunstler.[*]

I most wanted to be like Kunstler, still looking young and clean-cut in his mid-forties. Since 1961 when the ACLU had requested his help on behalf of the Freedom Riders, he had been coming down from New York. In 1964, Dr. King I think had asked him to represent the MFDP (Mississippi Freedom Democratic Party) in their struggle to unseat the recognized Mississippi delegation at the Democratic Party Convention. Bill was already the consummate trial lawyer, as likeable as he was bright and committed.

Bill got a little "out there" for my tastes in his later years, but back then to me he was another Clarence Darrow. When I met him he was wearing a dark blue suit, nothing fancy, but it fitted impeccably. I learned that women jurors like blue suits and that all men own at least one navy blue blazer in their lives. I confessed I could never be like him. He said it didn't matter, I should just be like myself. "Tell the stories," he said. "Look to the way your mother read stories to you as a child, with all the complexities, difficulties and joys."

---

[*] Tony Amsterdam was with the NAACP team. In 1972 he would successfully argue the Supreme Court death penalty case *Furman v. Georgia* that Gil mentions at the end of Chapter 17. Gil considered him that summer "the genius of the legal arm of the civil rights movement."

Kent Greenawalt had just finished a clerkship with Supreme Court Justice John M. Harlan. After the summer he continued on with the ACLU and other civil rights groups. A Columbia law professor since 1965, he has focused on constitutional law regarding church and state, freedom of speech, civil disobedience, and criminal responsibility.

Alan Levine, for over fifty years since Freedom Summer, has been a ground-level civil rights lawyer, argued before the Supreme Court, and taught constitutional litigation. His current work centers around Islamophobia, Palestinian justice and bigotry issues on college campuses.

Alvin Bronstein was an LCDC/National Lawyers Guild attorney. In 1966 he would win damages from a Mississippi deputy sheriff for a woman who had been beaten with a blackjack in jail, apparently the first time a Deep South law enforcement official was ordered to pay reparations for abusing a Black person. After the Attica prison riots of 1971, Bronstein focused on prisons. According to colleague Michele Deitch, "Al was responsible for almost all of the major prison reform class-action lawsuits around the country during the '70s, '80s and early '90s."

Most of the 800 arrested were held in cattle stockades at the Hinds County fairgrounds in Jackson, where conditions were worse than in the regular jails. I and others interviewed them and prepared many affidavits showing that the marches had been peaceful and that the police had responded with brutality. The affidavits were intended to be attached to motions to be presented to the federal court in an attempt to get the marchers released on bail, or might be used to support claims of rights to freedom of speech and the right to assemble.

We imposed a constant pressure on ourselves to get the prisoners out. We law students couldn't "practice law," but we worked from early morning until midnight, often forgetting breakfast or lunch. As requested, we wore suits and ties every day. We were clean-shaven with polished shoes as if we were working in establishment law offices.

It wasn't hard to find someone in the stockades to talk about police brutality. All the marchers had been forced to run through a gauntlet of police who beat them. Most blows had been aimed at places like the groin where the injuries would be less visible. I met a few young men who had been sent out to a hospital for stitches and then returned. Leaders were singled out for more intense beatings and then moved to the city jail. Each time a leader was taken, a new one would step forward.

Some of it was pretty random. Wayne Mercer of San Jose, California said, "I was in the chow line Wednesday. The officer told me that I was next, and before I knew what was happening he had hit me across the head with his billy club and knocked me down. He said, 'Next time move faster. Get to the back of the line.' So I got up and moved to the back of the line."

Our constraints in the stockades were basic: no recorders or cameras allowed; no chairs or tables, either. Laptops didn't yet exist. No interview rooms, unless you counted cattle stalls. No air-conditioning and often no roof as the Mississippi sun beat down. In time, the odor grew from the mass of human bodies with no shower facilities other than thunderstorms. With a pen and yellow legal pad, I would sit with one of the demonstrators on the concrete or dirt floor and pursue not a formula but a framework for conversation, writing down slowly and carefully, in their words, a little about who they were, what happened in the march, the facts of their arrest, what they had personally endured, and what they observed of the treatment of others. The demonstrators were bright people with relevant stories of their own to add. Before leaving I would recheck all facts with the client. Back at the office I would rewrite by hand to get it in proper sequence. One of our legal secretaries would type it up on a typewriter, carefully because the first draft was also the final. With it, I would return to the stockade for signing.

Surrounded by friends in the stockades, I was never afraid. My heart went out to some of the injured prisoners with whom I spoke. Our legal team was their only link to the outside world. Through us they could see that others on the outside were remembering them and working or praying for their release.

In retrospect, my experience in the Mississippi stockades may sound dismal. In fact it was exhilarating. Everyone there, be they lawyers, law students, arrested health workers, ministers, farmers, students, and other demonstrators, knew we were changing the world. It was hard, but no one really wanted to be outside, if their friends remained inside. People were singing and enjoying each other's company.

In the joyful and violent chaos, my one year of law school was essentially worthless. For a year I had sat in comfortable law school Socratic method classrooms being taught how to "think like a lawyer." I had never seen a client nor taken a statement. But a few minutes with John Doyle, who had finished Harvard Law School two years earlier, was all it took to bring me up to speed.

Well, I should revise the value of my one year of law school in one respect. I'd taken constitutional law with our Dean, Thomas M. Cooley, II, the epitome of an absent-minded professor but brilliant in his knowledge of that subject. When he wasn't probing our minds and making us think, Dean Cooley was wandering around the classroom on the 14th floor of Pitt's Cathedral of Learning, lecturing. Sometimes his wanders ended in one of the front corners of the gothic style classroom, standing there with his back to us, enraptured by the Constitution, lecturing to the ornate stonework, oblivious to our presence. I had strained to take in every word, which permitted me to see the broader picture of what was happening in the stockades.

I heard no complaints that we lawyers and law students couldn't get folks out yet. But I knew what was going on inside at times when we law students and lawyers were not allowed in and all the police had taped over their name tags.

In the stockades I interviewed Rev. J.C. Killingsworth from Enterprise, Mississippi. He was a tall, gentle, 44-year-old United Methodist minister who served a large number of small Black churches. By 1965 he had accumulated 23 years of ministry experience. He was a huge, fit man, both physically and spiritually. I took his statement on June 14. He had been at the head of the line of marchers in a dark suit carrying a sign that said, "We shall overcome." Across the street from the State Capitol Building he was stopped by a police officer.

Rev. Killingsworth related that the officer asked, "Do you have a permit for which to march?"

The reverend's response: "Yes. It was provided to me by the Constitution of the United States to march and peacefully to assemble to protest such things as we are not in keeping with, and I am sure you would not want to take away from us both our constitutional and God-given right."

Officer: "You are under arrest."

Rev. Killingsworth saw several of the demonstrators being beaten with sticks and kicked and thrown out of the high trucks by the Jackson City police. After they had been taken to a building at the stockades he saw others beaten with nightsticks by Mississippi highway patrolmen. Many were bloodied. Prisoners were required to sit on the stockade floor with legs drawn up. If anyone moved or made a sound they were beaten and cursed. Because Rev. Killingsworth had not been permitted to contact his wife, I took her a message that he was all right.

Rev. Ralph M. Galt was a 49-year-old United Church of Christ minister from Iowa in the last half of the line of about 400 marchers. At the arrest, one young man called for a prayer. Rev. Galt prayed in a loud voice for strength, guidance and justice for all in their group. Someone from another group suggested they sit down, but when arrested, all in their group went voluntarily into the trucks. When they were unloaded he could see persons being pulled out of the larger truck and being beaten with billies. The beatings continued in the fairgrounds. Rev. Galt was pushed with a billy club in the middle of his back. He saw a boy given a resounding blow to the head, sink to the floor and leave a pool of blood on the floor. After registration they were marched through a small door in single file where about fifteen policemen with clubs struck and poked almost every prisoner. Rev. Galt received a blow on the head which swelled up to about the size of a 50-cent piece.

On June 21, I heard James Forman speak at the Shrine Hall. Since 1961, Forman had been the executive secretary of SNCC. His was the famous quip, "If we can't sit at the table of democracy, let's knock the fucking legs off!" He was sometimes referred to as one of the "Big Five" civil rights leaders, meeting regularly with Dr. King of the SCLC (Southern Christian Leadership Conference), James Farmer of CORE (Congress of Racial Equality), Roy Wilkins (NAACP), Whitney Young, Jr. (Urban League) to coordinate movement strategies. Forman was a returning local boy, having spent his early years with his grandmother on a farm in Marshall County.*

Next morning I met with Forman to prepare for the legal defense before his expected arrest (along with 73 others) in another of the series of marches toward the Capitol over the voting rights issue.

I watched it all from across the street. The people came two-by-two down the sidewalk from the Morning Star Church in an orderly silent march. The cops (at least fifty, maybe a hundred) formed a line across North Farish near the Lawyers' Committee office. They had been waiting there with the sanitation department trucks, large cages on wheels.

The marchers stopped and moved off the sidewalk into a vacant lot where Mrs. Annie Devine spoke to them about the right to vote. Annie Devine had quit her job selling insurance in Canton, Mississippi, to work full-time for CORE. She was also an elected representative within the MFDP which challenged the legitimacy of the white-only regular Democratic Party.

Then the cops came down the center of the street, about thirty of them, all marching in step. An officer announced that everyone would be arrested for an "unlawful assembly." The cops surrounded the group and everyone in the group sat down. The cops picked them up off the ground and dropped them. They dragged them across the cement walk and asphalt street and threw them into the trucks. I was surprised to see a cop land a fast kick on a boy who was on the ground. Usually they did that stuff away from the view of reporters.

The arrests included four 11-to-12-year-old children who had been watching from too close by and were sent off to the stockades. A secretary from our office was arrested. She had more courage than I did, but I rationalized that my job was to help people get back out of jail.

There was very little press coverage of the marches and mass arrests. The northern news media had seen similar marches in Jackson the prior summer and in Selma that spring. My guess is they had de-

---

*Age 37 in 1965, he was older than many in SNCC.

cided that marches were no longer news. Now things had been esca-
lated. Now it took the deaths of white civil rights workers to interest
the press. Admittedly, covering civil rights events in Mississippi was
not easy work. When photographers or television cameramen got in
close to the action, they were likely to lose their equipment and film to
the police or aggressive whites. They could lose much more if they
fought to keep it. Sometimes they would shoot a good image, then
take off running.

As the arrests went on, I was sent to the state capitol to research
voting rights cases in its law library, which was much more extensive
than our own back at the office. Ironically I seemed to be the only one
who made it to the capitol grounds. All marchers were arrested before
they got there. Among other things I found a decision from the Fifth
Circuit Court of Appeals which said that Negroes are allowed to vote
in Mississippi. I liked the last sentence: "The mandate of this court
shall issue forthwith." If only Jackson was hiring literate police officials....

In southern style, once arrested, the white women were treated differently. About fifty were separated from the other prisoners at the
fairgrounds and put in the jail. Nancy Sours of Oakton, Virginia, told
me:

> "When they tried to take us out (from the fairgrounds) we re-
> fused and they dragged us out again by our feet. Everything
> you heard about the Jackson Police is true. They are brutal
> people. There have been a lot of beatings and as a matter of
> fact one of the girls in my cell has five stitches in her forehead
> one of the charming local police hit her for no reason. There
> was a woman (at the fairground) yesterday who is three
> months pregnant, and she got beaten. She's very sick and they
> won't even bring her to the hospital."

I interviewed Emily Gordon from Ann Arbor, Michigan in the
Jackson City Jail. She'd been working in the COFO office in Jackson.
She'd been about a third of the way back in a group of about 400 people, marching two-by-two and holding hands. She went peacefully
and was loaded into a paddy wagon with about twelve others. Inside
the wagon was very hot, and they pleaded for air. As they walked into
the fairgrounds a Mississippi highway patrolman jabbed a boy named
Bruce Maxwell with his nightstick. Noticing that she'd witnessed this,
the patrolman struck her across the forehead. She immediately began
to bleed and could see nothing for two or three minutes because of the
blood in her eyes. Linda Dugas, one of the nurses who had also been

arrested, helped her to lie down and gave first aid including a small bandage. Later Emily was taken to the University Medical Center where she received five stitches for the cut in her head. Returned to the fairgrounds, she was then taken to the city jail at about 5:00.

Emily also witnessed a highway patrolman charge a small group of people with his billy club, saying, "Move back." As they were backing up he struck Bill Light over the head with the club. Bill fell to the ground unconscious. He was bleeding profusely but no one from the group was allowed to give him aid. He was finally moved to an area separate from the other prisoners and not allowed to return to the prison group. He was not given medical help until an ambulance arrived about fifteen minutes later.[*]

From Vivianne Green of Pleasant Hill, California, who was in the Jackson city jail, I took this statement:

> "Yesterday at noon we started fasting in protest at the arrest (illegal, they said we needed a Jackson City permit to demonstrate and we already have the Constitution of the United States, the only permit necessary). We also resent the fact that all us white girls are in a relatively comfortable jail and the rest of the people in the movement are stuck in the unventilated barns at the local fairgrounds, where the brutality rate increases."

Marjorie Hahn from San Francisco described the jailing:

> "We sleep on bare, filthy mattresses, the cockroaches prowl the walls and the floor. They punish us for singing by shutting the air vents so it is hot, humid and ventless. In case you can't tell, I'm in very good shape spiritually. I'm getting a little weak and lightheaded from fasting (2 days now) but the kids are great and the songs are terrific."

The prisoners sang newer words to old spirituals and freedom songs, including these to the tune of a labor song, "Which side are you on?":

> *Father was a freedom fighter. I am freedom's son They say that in Hinds County, there are no neutrals there.*

---

[*] Bill was a young Stanford engineering graduate who'd joined SNCC/COFO in Mississippi in spring 1964. This was his fourth arrest. Looking back fifty years later he wrote, "During my time in MS, I experienced many of the high and low points of my life, met some of the most important people in my life, learned important lessons, and, like many of us, left feeling discouraged, and questioning whether anything important had been accomplished. It took many years for me to see the fruits of our work, but now I think the importance of what we did is quite obvious."

> *You're either a freedom fighter or a Tom for Ross Barnett.*[†]
> *Come all you bargain Northerners, with all your excess fat.*
> *30 days in the Jackson Jail will sure get rid of that.*
> *Don't Tom for Mr. Charley. Don't listen to his lies,*
> *We ain't gonna win this battle, unless we organize....*

And these to the tune of the spiritual "I'm Going to Sit at the Welcome Table," which blues singer Brownie McGhee had further popularized as "I'm Going to Tell God How You Treat Me":

> *I'm gonna walk the streets of freedom*
> *I'm gonna walk the streets of freedom one of these days,*
> *Hallelujah!*
> *I'm gonna walk the streets of freedom*
> *Gonna walk the streets of freedom one of these days.*
>
> *I'm gonna be a registered voter*
> *I'm gonna be a registered voter one of these days,*
> *Hallelujah!....*
> *I'm gonna sleep with the Governor's daughter*
> *I'm gonna sleep with the Governor's daughter one of these days,*
> *Hallelujah!....*

The prisoners weren't necessarily unanimous about the appropriateness of all these verses. The Mississippi church ladies there in the stockades never would have approved of the last.

I went to the stockade gate and asked to see Mrs. Divens.

A cop at the gate looked in his book and said, "We ain't got no Mrs. Divens."

"She must be there," I said, "I saw her yesterday and no one has been let out."

He asked if I was from Jackson. I said I came from Pittsburgh.

To that he said, "I don't know how you do things there, but when you introduce a n----- lady you don't say Mrs. Divens, you say n----- Divens. I want that understood. That's what the Bible calls them."

Since I wanted to get in, I didn't talk back. I could hear my mother often repeating wisdom passed on by the rabbit Thumper in Disney's "Bambi": "If you can't say nothin' nice, don't say nothin' at all."

Knowing what was happening inside, all civil rights lawyers in Jackson worked frantically and cooperatively to get the demonstrators out

---

[†] Governor of Mississippi, 1960-1964.

of jail. Starting on the day of the first arrests, injunctive actions were filed in Federal District Court by NAACP lawyer Marian Wright (later Edelman) against the arrest and prosecution of demonstrators.[*]

I didn't see how she could have done this so quickly unless she had drafted the lawsuits before the demonstrations happened. Marian had a wonderful ability to see and plan for the future. Federal District Judge Harold Cox, who seemed to do everything possible to oppose civil rights, delayed holding a hearing and, after it was held, delayed his decision while each day more voting rights demonstrators were carted off to jail. As he knew, it's hard to appeal a decision before it is made. Usually a case can be appealed only after a formal decision is signed by the trial judge.

Still, as Cox delayed, wise old John Honnold got to talking with Melvyn Zarr, a lawyer two years out of Harvard, saying, "Maybe the failure to make a decision could be a decision in itself."

"Justice delayed is justice denied?" Zarr responded. He'd begun his career with civil rights work in Mississippi and was now attached to the Mississippi office of the NAACP, Inc., Fund. His words were more a statement of hope than of a legal principle. "What if we filed a petition with the Fifth Circuit letting them know what is happening with the delay by Judge Cox?" he added presciently.[†]

"Not a likely winner," said Honnold, "but I don't see how it could hurt."

So along with Marian they set to work on the petition.[‡]

On June 28, they sought review from Judge John Minor Wisdom of the Fifth Circuit Court of Appeals. An emergency panel of three appellate judges was convened who, in only two days and without hearing, issued an order that the demonstrators be allowed to march two abreast, with or without posters, on the sidewalks of Jackson, Mississippi and be allowed to distribute handbills. This provided

---

[*] Marian was 23, two years out of Yale Law School.

[†] After almost seven years of intense civil rights lawyering, Melvyn worked on poverty law reform in Massachusetts, then joined the faculty at the University of Maine School of Law. In an insightful, pithy "Recollections of My Time in the Civil Rights Movement" (*Maine Law Review*, 61:2, Article 3. June 2009), he concludes of his civil rights work that his "greatest point of pride" was not having "screwed up—a very weighty and powerful ambition—especially in light of the stakes."

[‡] For a more focused higher level synopsis of legal steps taken after the mass arrests, see the LCCRUL "Report on the Committee Office in the South, June 2 - August 6, 1965," filed by Executive Director Berl I. Bernhard. Contact *lawyerscommittee.org*.

some protection against future arrests but didn't free the 800 already jailed.

If you want to know something about the political views of a federal district court judge, one place to look is the senator who backed their nomination. By tradition, the President would nominate someone selected by a senator of the President's political party from the state where the vacancy had occurred. Judge Cox had been selected by Mississippi Senator James Eastland, then chair of the Senate Judiciary Committee. Eastland had said that no one needed to obey the Supreme Court's 1954 school desegregation decision, *Brown v. Board of Education*, and had also told President Johnson that (before their remains were discovered) the disappearance of Chaney, Goodman and Schwerner was a "publicity stunt." Cox and Eastland had been roommates at Ole Miss. It was pretty clear from the start that Cox was an ultraconservative southerner. In a voting rights case a year before these latest arrests, Judge Cox had referred to a group of Negro witnesses as a "bunch of chimpanzees." This had caused a big fuss in Congress and a proposal to impeach him, but nothing came of it. As a federal judge, Cox was on the bench for life. We could grumble about him behind his back but had to treat him with the same respect due any federal judge. Our only advantage was that the appellate judges on the United States Fifth Circuit Court of Appeals knew Judge Cox at least as well as we did.*

I began to see that law on paper is one thing. In reality, it lives in the hearts and minds of people. The Fifth Circuit judges were playing a major role in the legal advances of the civil rights movement. Judge John Minor Wisdom was one of those who, usually in panels of three, consistently overruled Cox in these cases. Judge Wisdom had been a lawyer and adjunct law professor at Tulane University in New Orleans. He had helped Eisenhower win Louisiana in the presidential election.

Most of the demonstrators were held on $100 bail, some $200. This was a huge sum for a Mississippi sharecropper of that time. Those freedom fighters who might have been able to afford the bail were determined not to leave until everyone else was also released. One of my jobs was to do research for a petition for people's release on their own recognizance; that is, without posting bail bonds. In essence, we would argue that, since they were unconstitutionally

---

* Melvyn Zarr recollects that Kennedy accommodated Eastland's choice in exchange for Eastland's okay of Kennedy's appointment of Thurgood Marshall to the federal bench.

charged with minor offences, they were unlikely to run away before trial and should be released without posting bail. But motions we filed in both state and federal court were rejected or simply ignored. Finally, an anonymous donor put up $40,000 to secure the release of all the adult demonstrators by the end of June.

We filed other petitions to remove the state prosecutions to federal court, which were rejected by the clerk of the Federal District Court based on a local rule, ordered to be accepted for filing by the Fifth Circuit, and again rejected by the clerk. The court never ruled on them. One issue was whether a joint petition could be filed or whether we needed to file some 800 petitions separately notarized by each demonstrator. In those days before typewriters were computers, the demonstrators had been released on bail and the right to march had been won before we could file that many petitions.

Besides adults, we needed to secure the release of minors. Black Mississippi boys and girls were hoping to grow up free in their own state rather than fleeing north. This aspiration was rooted in their homes, families, churches and the American dream. Staying in Mississippi and changing the system were also explicitly encouraged in the Freedom Schools, many of which had been organized during the 1964 Freedom Summer project, with a professionally designed curriculum that combined education in reading and writing with the works of inspirational Black authors.

Children were often more eager than the adults to join in the demonstrations. About forty percent of the 800 arrested in the Jackson Voting Rights marches were children. The entire Steptoe family from Pike County in southern Mississippi came to march in Jackson and was thrown in jail. Mr. Steptoe said they came "because the MFDP (Mississippi Freedom Democratic Party) is the one hope my youngsters have, not to have to live like I had to for so long."

The Youth Court judge for Hinds County, which includes Jackson, was Carl Guernsey. Judge Guernsey followed the usual procedure of individual delinquency hearings for each child, generally with a parent present, before they would be considered for release.[*]

---

[*] The youngest arrested (by Officer Kohler, for refusing to let go of a small American flag) was five- or six-year-old Anthony Quinn. With a Ph.D in education, Anthony later found his career in school administration. To his credit, Kohler's family, after his death, said that he had regretted that moment "for the rest of his life."

Anthony Quinn had been sitting next to MCHR doctor June
Finer. Both were arrested.

Jackson arrestees hauled into a cage truck, June 24, 1965.
Photos by journalist and former Freedom Rider Matt Herron.

A 35-year-old Lawyers' Committee volunteer, GWU law professor James Starrs, represented or coordinated the representation of more than 350 children. I helped Jim with such matters as procuring suitable clothing to wear at hearings and bus tickets for parents to come to court.[†]

It was a long and slow process. Many of the children were prisoners in the stockades for two weeks or more before they got their hearings. Release of the children was dependent on the Judge's determination, not on posting bail, so the $40,000 bail fund did not help the young detainees. Some of the children got their hearings and were released before the adults. Each child and parent had to understand the legal standards that would be applied by the judge for release. Each had to be carefully prepared for questions from the prosecutor and judge. Generally the children were released to their parents if they promised not to break "valid" laws against demonstrating in the future. Jim and the other volunteer lawyers would explain to each child that laws that violate constitutional rights are not "valid." It was a delicate dance.

Sometimes it was hard to contact a parent or get them in to court, either from Jackson or remoter parts. Occasionally, Judge Guernsey would allow release to a responsible adult other than a parent. In a few cases, usually when the child had a prior charge of delinquency, Guernsey sent children to the Oakley Training School, a segregated Negro reformatory, and the civil rights lawyers continued to work for their release.

In conjunction with the marches on the capital for voting rights, leaflets were handed out announcing meetings to protest the special legislative session. An MFDP leaflet called for a protest against:

The Gathering on Monday of Mississippi Lawmakers
The Illegally Elected State Legislators
MASS RALLY Tonight 8:30 pm
Morning Star Baptist Church, Kane St., Off Mill

[†] In a subsequent academic career, Starrs specialized in forensic evidence, often applying science to persisting riddles about identities or causes of death. Among other cases, he studied the Boston Strangler, Jesse James, Jay Edgar Hoover, Sacco and Vanzetti, and the Lindbergh kidnapping.

Gil on an errand to the Jackson MFDP office. *Photo by Marian Wright Edelman.*

Handing it out, Garland Strother* and others were arrested and charged with violating a Jackson ordinance that prohibited distributing handbills, posters, dodgers and other like objects unless a permit was obtained from the city council and a bond posted in an amount fixed by the council.

To me, the ordinance clearly was an unconstitutional prior restraint on free speech. We removed the cases prosecuting the leafleters to Federal District Court. It rejected our freedom-of-speech claims and upheld the ordinance. It took a while, but the Fifth Circuit Court of Appeals reversed, declaring it unconstitutional on February 14, 1967.

---

* Possibly Louisiana native Garland Strother, five years out of college. Later on he became a widely published poet and a highly regarded librarian.

5. *Love in a Dangerous Time*

The work on the arrests and releases continued through half of July. In rare, off-work hours* one could go to some local bars, but this was always embarrassing. Seeing my skin, some local gentleman, perhaps with a little too much to drink, would treat me as a hero and buy me a beer, ignoring the experienced Black SNCC worker with me. So what little free time we had, we spent at (Mrs.) Steven's Kitchen, a local hangout on Farish for civil rights activists. There, lunch could be had for 50 cents and a complete dinner for 90 cents. I seldom could afford that and so usually ate at the apartment.

Steven's Kitchen, years after its closing.
Photo courtesy of Susan C. Allen.

In that sweltering Mississippi summer, one ice cold beer was 50 cents. On my very tight budget, beer was a luxury that just couldn't make it. Not if I wanted to eat.

I was hanging out in Steven's Kitchen one evening, in my suit and tie as usual.† Four Black SNCC organizers were there, a girl and three

---

* From typically 80-hour weeks.

† Out in rural Mississippi and not working for the Lawyers' Committee, Lizcrick's Mel Leventhal went tieless, dressing like a civil rights worker.

young men. At least they looked like SNCC to me, wearing white dress shirts, overalls or dark slacks. One of the guys called out to me:

"Hey, white boy, we're busted. Buy a round of beers."

"You think because I'm wearing a coat and tie, I've got some money." I said. "These are just my work clothes. You wouldn't want your lawyer to try to defend you in Levi's."

"You ain't old enough to be no damn lawyer."

"You got me there." I replied. "I'm a lowly law student."

"You're jus' a lowly asshole," he replied. It wasn't exactly a welcome, but the tone of voice and slouched body language didn't seem hostile.

The girl got up from their table and sat down across from me.

"I'm Thelma." She was about nineteen, very pretty, with medium brown skin and, like the guys, a natural Afro hairdo cut short. There haven't been many times in my life when a girl as beautiful as Thelma Hill sat down at my table.[*]

"I'm a peacekeeper," she said, loudly enough for her comrades to hear. Then to me in a softer voice, "They're all pacifists. Followers of Gandhi." Her words relieved me of my fear that tensions would escalate.

"Since y'all are in Steven's Kitchen, a white law student in Steven's Kitchen, I bet you're doin' sompin in the movement? 'Sup?"

"I'm working with Lizcrick." I said. "Mostly I've been working on getting people out of jail. There still are some juveniles we're trying to get out."

"Perhaps y'all helped get me out." she said.

"No. If I had met you, even in that mass of people, I'm sure I would have remembered."

"Why are some still in jail?" she asked.

"Well, you know the drill. In that dance with the judge, some kids just can't say the right words about not demonstrating 'illegally' no matter how carefully they are prepared."

"Yeah," she said, "That lawyer, Jim, insisted on going through all that. I tol' him I knew it all already."

I went on to tell how kids who had pending juvenile charges for shoplifting or similar things should not have been in the march. She responded by admitting she and others working for SNCC and COFO needed to give them a heads-up on that risk.

[‡] Most likely this was 1964 Freedom Summer SNCC volunteer Thelma J. Hill. In mid-July Gil thought she was 17.

From there on, Thelma told me a lot, helping me sort out all the confusing acronyms for various parts of the movement, saying how in Mississippi SNCC and COFO were pretty much interchangeable terms, though the former, she said with a glow, came nearer to expressing the spiritual side and its youth who did most of the work. Strictly speaking COFO was an umbrella for SNCC and "older, 'more mature'" groups like the NAACP, Farmer's CORE and King's SCLC. COFO had been formed to help them get money from institutions like the Field, Taconic, New World, and Stern Family foundations. President Kennedy's team had helped get foundation support, routed through a related umbrella called the Voter Education Project.

She said, "Kennedy didn't want to see us upsetting people with freedom rides and 'sit ins' in diners. He thought that voter registration would be less controversial. He didn't know how wrong he could be."

At age 17 in 1962, she'd attended the very first meeting of COFO, held in Clarksdale Mississippi, and had dropped out of high school to join it.

She seemed to gaze back to the "distant" past: "Mos' of us were from SNCC. Mos' leadership roles went to the older leaders: Aaron Henry from the NAACP was elected president, Rev. R.L.T. Smith was treasurer and the lawyer, Carsie Hall, was secretary. Jim Farmer's CORE kids took the area around Meridian, but Bob Moses from SNCC was appointed the COFO statewide project director and Bob become the real leader."[*]

"I keep hearing about Bob Moses without ever seeing him," I said. "What's up?"

"Don't know," she said, "He's the mos' kind and gentle person. Heading voter registration work in 'Sippi was hard. They jail and beat SNCC workers. Bob's SNCC workers. When Bob's COFO workers brought folk in to register they would be beaten. Bob, too, of course. But he suffered more from what happened to others than what happened to himself. The deaths of Chaney, Goodman and Schwerner, COFO/CORE kids, his kids, hit him hard.[†] Him with his

---

[*] Thelma was reflecting the disdain of young, grassroots SNCC campaigners for Henry and Smith's connections with the NAACP and its seemingly slower legalistic approach. Among other things, Rev. Smith in 1961 had been the first African American to run for Congress since Reconstruction.

[†] Interestingly, Aaron Henry says it was his own encounter with Andrew Goodman that cemented Andrew's decision to go south.

Coke bottle glasses, he always looks fragile, but he's tough as rawhide. Maybe he went back."

"Back where ?" I asked.

"To Harvard."

"That's my little brother's school," I bragged. "What was Bob Moses' tie to Harvard?"

"A master's degree in philosophy. He lives by Camus, the existentialist. 'I rebel, therefore we exist.' He turned me on to *The Rebel* and *The Plague*."

"That's heavy reading for a child."

"A chil'?" she said. "I never was a chil'. I've always been a chil'."

She asked what had brought me to Mississippi. I confessed that Alan's going south this summer to do voter registration work had left me no excuse for staying at home. I didn't mention Lisa Marshall. No need to complicate things. I felt that Thelma was a kindred spirit. Our eyes and minds connected even when nothing was said. They say that men are attracted to women like their mothers. In appearance Thelma was a lot like Mattie. But she had the fire of the movement in her and was experienced way beyond her age.

She asked where Alan was and said she'd like to meet him.

It was good to be able to say he was in South Carolina. There was always the risk a favorite girl might prefer him to me.

I asked how voter registration work was going now. I understood voter registration to be the main focus of COFO, although it also helped with creating Freedom Schools, Freedom Houses and related activities.

Actually, Thelma confided, it had been so unsuccessful at registering voters in Mississippi in 1963 for the 1964 Presidential election that the funding it had received for this via the Voter Registration Project* had been redirected more productively to border states like Tennessee and Kentucky.

Various factors had undermined registration drives in Mississippi. Besides the poll tax and the complex tests, often would-be registrants could not even enter the courthouse. Sheriffs would arrest everyone on the steps outside and charge them with "parading without a permit" or "unlawful assembly."

"Folks knew the risks," she told me, "and wouldn't go down except for a brave few in the company of the SNCC leader. The SNCC leader

---

* Gil may mean the *Voter Education Project*.

would be beaten in jail. The others arrested would be identified to the White Citizens Council or some such group. All in their families would lose their jobs. To anyone who actually made it into the court-house to register, an official would give an impossibly dense section of the Mississippi Constitution to interpret. Then fail them no matter what their answer. Of course, unless they were white."

"What did you do without funding?" I asked.

"Don't worry yourself. We just ate a little less and some took on part-time jobs."

Thelma described past lack of success at official voter registration not as a failure but as a step in the learning process that caused Bob Moses to develop a different strategy of voter education. Rather than futilely attempting to register at courthouses, he had shifted to the idea of "registering" for what was called The Freedom Vote, mainly in the Mississippi Delta, wherever that was (at the time I mistakenly thought she meant the river's mouth at the Gulf). In this process, in Black churches there and elsewhere, 73,000 Black people registered and then voted without danger in an unofficial election. Unofficial though it was, it demonstrated the will of the people to vote, getting ready for the real election of 1964.

"I didn't know all that was going on in the Delta. All I knew was that Muddy Waters and Howlin' Wolf came from there."

"You got good taste." she said.

"Who do you like?"

"Sam Cooke."

"*A change is gonna come*," I said, quoting the song of his that had become a popular anthem for the movement shortly before Cooke died.*

"*Been a long time comin',*" she continued the lyric. "Too bad he won't be here to see it."

I was glad that we seemed to be making some connection through the music

Now, with passage pending of the 1965 voting rights act, she said, COFO was shifting back to real voter registration in Mississippi.

"What's South Carolina like?" I asked.

"I don't know," she said, "But I'll pray for your little brother."

That didn't make me feel any better. "It can't be like Mississippi." I said.

"No. It's not."

---

* Born in Clarksdale, Mississippi, Cooke died in December 1964.

Getting back to the gaps in my local understanding, I asked where the Mississippi Freedom Democratic Party fit into all this. For Thelma, the MFDP had started out as just "different letters" for SNCC and COFO. Founded in April 1964 by Bob Moses and two SNCC field secretaries, Fannie Lou Hamer and Larry Guyot, it was born of the fact that SNCC couldn't get large numbers of Blacks registered as official Mississippi State voters.[†] The MFDP shifted focus to a national level (the national Democratic Party) where rules and pre-occupations were different. The national body held the power to decide who could sit at its national convention. MFDP was presenting itself as a non-exclusionary alternative to the existing all-white Mississippi delegation. Last year's Freedom Summer had recruited students from the North for the MFDP's voter registration drive.

The rest had been covered on national TV. In August 1964, a racially integrated group of 68 elected delegates from the MFDP challenged the all-white regular Mississippi Democratic Party delegation and applied to be seated at the Democratic National Convention in Atlantic City. There Fannie Lou Hamer's speech stirred the country. She talked about her childhood as a sharecropper, the barriers for Blacks to vote in Mississippi, and the murders of Medgar Evers, James Chaney, Andrew Goodman, and Michael Schwerner. She vividly described how she had been beaten for attending a civil rights meeting.

In the end only two seats were offered to the MFDP—and rejected. But the message of segregation of the regular Mississippi Democratic Party and of voting rights discrimination in Mississippi had been delivered. In turn, this had added momentum for the still-pending *Voting Rights Act of 1965*.

I asked Thelma if she'd like to go dancing.

"You're very nice," she said, "I wouldn't want to be unfaithful to the young Black men who are working in the movement."

I never gave up trying, but she always kept our friendship on a businesslike basis.

It was the time of the sexual revolution. "The pill" had been licensed by the Food and Drug Administration in 1960. It had been a

---

[†] Hamer and Guyot are both well remembered for their leading roles in civil rights. In 1966 Guyot became an anti-war candidate for Congress, in 1971 a lawyer, and in 1978 an election campaigner for Marion Barry. He was also a close friend of anti-war boxer Muhammad Ali. More about him in Chapter 9.

factor in the changing attitudes about sex. Many young people were shifting away from old uptight values, particularly those active in the movement. It seemed like there was an unexpressed feeling that if you are risking death, you might as well live first. AIDS was still unheard of. Of course, you raised your death risks quite a bit if the Mississippi cops caught you dating across the color line.

I did find a girlfriend in Jackson. Slender, very pretty, Willow had ebony skin that glowed, a round face framed in carefully styled, medium-length hair that curved around her face in front and puffed up in back.

She dressed well, as if she borrowed concepts of form and simplicity from Jackie Kennedy. She wore dresses or skirts and tops, not jeans, but that was normal for girls at that time. Of course she couldn't afford designer versions. I suspect she made her chic outfits in home economics class or on a friend's sewing machine. In any case she looked good.

And she had lips that looked like, well, lips.

Real lips didn't run in the old, white, Welsh Venable line. A few years later my brother Alan told me about a tiny African-American kid who'd walked up to him in West Philadelphia, pointed and said, "Man, you got a small mouth!" Like Alan, I have a small mouth, but Willow seemed to like me in spite of that.

In those days every girl seemed to smell different. Willow smelled like peaches and pine needles. I'm surprised to still remember that unique scent.

What I liked best was the way she talked. There was something musical in her speech. She sometimes spoke in popular lyrics, at other times just rhymed as if her words had come from songs.

She and her girlfriends hung out around the civil rights law offices on Farish, so I thought she was involved in the movement. I had gotten to know her just through glances and "Good mornings." One day she and her friends were making noise in our library and Professor Honnold chased them out. "This is a place for work," he told me.

Willow and I found ourselves alone together one evening as I was leaving the office.

"What's goin' on?" she asked me.

I said something dumb, like, "I'm working on a writ of habeas corpus."

"No, I mean does you ever do anything fun?"

I stopped myself from saying "That *is* what I do for fun." Instead I said, "What would your mother think?"

"My Momma died in a knife fight in a bar when I was very little," she said.

"What about your father?"

"I never knew him. My gramma raised me."

"That must have been hard," I said.

"Anyway, Gramma will always love me."

We walked for a little while. I tried to think of something to say. News of progress on implementing the *Civil Rights Act of 1964* had been on the radio. Bobby Kennedy was running for the Senate.

"Bobby Kennedy must be proud about the civil rights act progress," I said.

"I thought his name was John," she said. "I saw him on TV. He was cute. You never know a good thing 'til it's gone."

"True," I said, not wanting to embarrass her.

"Do you have a girlfriend up North?" she asked.

"I might." It was not much of a confession.

"Tell it like it is," she said, "I'm not the jealous type."

"Not really," I said. "There's a girl I like, but she doesn't seem to like me."

"I'm not jealous of a maybe," she said.

I was thinking of her hard life and how little opportunity it offered her. Mississippi was at or below the bottom of the American barrel on measures of poverty, education and unemployment. "You must want to get out of Mississippi," I said.

"Like a long lonely stream, I keep runnin' towards a dream," she said. "All I want is a family in a little home with a white picket fence."

We walked slowly in the hot night, heading nowhere in particular. My hand brushed hers in the darkness. She didn't move away. I made what for me was a brave move and took her soft hand as we walked. As we came to a church, she said, "That's Morning Star, my gramma's church."

"Was it once yours?"

"Still is, I guess," she said. "I just don't go much anymore."

We stopped in the dark by the church. I pulled her hand gently and Willow spiraled against me. As I put my arms around her, her tight, muscular body melted. And there was her face. Her face and her mouth, an inch away from mine. What else could I do? It was soft, warm and gentle. We clung together for what seemed like the length of a song. Then we floated down the street, silently continuing our walk.

After a while Willow asked, "Would y'all like to meet my gramma?"
"Sure."

We walked a few blocks to a tiny apartment in an old neighborhood with large pecan trees and a little grass. Willow's gramma was surprisingly young, not like the white-haired, frail grandmas I was used to.

As usual, I was wearing a suit. Willow introduced me as her friend and said I worked in the civil rights movement.

We sat on the two small beds, because there were no chairs. A small table stood in the corner with a two-burner hotplate. A little sink served both the kitchen corner and bathroom. The room was partly below ground, with only one narrow window high up over a tiny TV. A screen door provided ventilation. On one wall hung a quilt. A few family photos hung on the other wall, along with the pictures of two white men, Jesus and John F. Kennedy. I had learned not to say that Jesus of Nazareth had certainly had dark skin and hair.

Gramma pointed to one of the family photos: "This was Willow's mama, my daughter Jimmella." The girl in the photo was about Willow's age. It looked like a high school photo.

"She was pretty," I said.

"Yes, but a lot of trouble," said Gramma.

The one thing of beauty in the apartment was a crazy quilt with multicolored patches that varied in size and shape. The stitches holding the piecework together were intricate and none the same. Looking closely I saw tiny pictures embroidered here and there.

"That took a lot of work. It's beautiful."

"Apart from Willow, it's the best thing I have," said Gramma. "My grandmother made it."

Gramma took my hands in hers. Her hands were hard and rough from work.

"You're a gentleman," she said. "Take good care of my Willow."

"I will."

One night, Willow and I double-dated with a Black law student and his white wife. I had been assigned the management of our stable of rented cars and was allowed to check one out for personal use, as long as I didn't break the rental contract by leaving the state. More to impress Willow than for its performance characteristics, I picked out a black Ford Thunderbird V-8.

We drove out of Hinds County for some great music. Designed for privacy, the club was situated on a small island in a lake. You could get to it only by driving down a narrow dirt causeway. Anyone coming, including the sheriff, could be seen way in advance. It was an old place, perhaps once a speakeasy. In its friendly atmosphere our troubles melted. We relaxed and danced to live rhythm and blues. On the way home I saw many red flashing lights ahead — an accident or police roadblock. At night in Mississippi, no way could interracial pairs stop for a roadblock.

Life is best in a V-8 Ford with a beautiful girl, running from the Mississippi police. I turned off the lights, pulled onto a side road and floored it. The car lurched forward, pressing the four of us into the backs of our seats. I was motivatin' down the road and nothing could touch my low-slung '65 T-bird with 345 horsepower under the hood. Like a chicken fleeing a wolf, we streaked up the road. In the rutted dirt, the steering wheel took on a life of its own. I hung on, trying to keep the car straight as we slammed through occasional patches of mud that drummed against the undercarriage, shook the car and splashed out both sides.

A quarter moon gave just enough light to see a dirt crossroad heading our way. I took my foot off the gas to slow down without triggering the rear brake lights. I managed a fishtail turn at the cross. I hit the gas and we raced back in the general direction we had come. Finally in the distance to the left I saw a clump of scraggly pines. We turned onto a rutted cow path and crept slowly up it into the trees where I stopped.

Willow trembled next to me. We sat in the dark woods hoping we had not been seen and waited while the monster engine cooled. After a while we got out. We stood in the muggy night air with stars above, looking out in the distance for flashing red lights.

No one came.

We had violated all of Marian Wright's well founded rules of safety, so I consoled myself with the thought that my actual supervisor wasn't she but John Doyle. I looked over at the mud-caked sides of the T-bird. I'd need to return this car to the rental agency before Prof. Honnold saw it. With headlights back on and at conservative speeds, we took back lanes around the roadblock and back to Jackson.

Willow was back the next evening.

"You doin' okay?" I asked.

"You're somethin' else," she said, "*You came into my heart, so tenderly.*" What else can you do?"

---

* The Supremes, 1964.

"It's a fast life," I said.

"I wanna talk to you, say sweet things to you. *Come on boy, see about me.*"

"Your talk is like music," I said.

"Ain't nothing like the real thing," she said, "*so bring your sweet loving, bring it on home to me.*"

"I think I hear a little Sam Cooke," I said. "Do you like 'A Change is Gonna Come?'"

"Sure," Willow said, "but I live for today."

I made an attempt to play the game. "*Another day, another night, I long to hold you tight.*"[†]

She smiled but did not criticize. "*Well if you feel like lovin' me, I second that emotion.*"[‡]

She dreamt of a home and children just as did other girls I had dated. But they weren't my dreams. My dreams were the movement.

[†] The Four Tops, 1964.

[‡] Gil's memory lets him down here with this *1967* Miracles' song.

6. Dismantling Mississippi Segregation

I had been in Mississippi for about a month. With the pace slowed down following the victory in the Court of Appeals, we turned to other cases. They involved me in so many civil rights issues that the stories in this book amount nearly to an introduction to civil rights law. For those who want a deeper look, I recommend reading the Supreme Court cases mentioned. The opinions are easily found on the internet by searching on the case citation number, for example "347 US 463."

As I've said, I'd ridden south with other law students, including Mel Leventhal. Mel was assigned to the NAACP, Inc., Fund to work primarily on desegregation of schools. He later returned for a long career as a Mississippi civil rights lawyer and along the way married Alice Walker, later Pulitzer Prize winning author of *The Color Purple.**

One weekday afternoon or evening Mel and I drove north from Jackson to meet with the members of a black Baptist church who were interested in integrating a white public school. Marian Wright had wanted to take the case but didn't have time to drive up for the meeting. She sent Mel, who seemed to know the Old Testament better than I did and had a wonderful rapport with the local Black Baptists. I tagged along because we always tried to avoid driving out into the Delta alone.

The law that supported integration of schools found its source in the Constitution, rather than in statutes passed by Congress. Racial segregation violates the 14th amendment, which provides that no state shall "deny to any person within its jurisdiction the equal protection of the laws." Today we might find it self-evident that this language prohibits segregation. But in 1896 the Supreme Court, in *Plessy v. Ferguson* (163 US 537), held that "separate but equal" was okay. The reality that followed was separate and unequal schools. The 1954 Supreme Court decision in *Oliver L. Brown et al. v. the Board of Education of Topeka (KS) et al.* (347 US 483) overturned the *Plessy*

---

* While living in Mississippi they were its only interracial marriage. At the end of summer 1965, Lawyer's Committee attorney Rick Abel praised Mel's having single-handedly and without facilities maintained a field office bolstering the movement in Holmes County in the Delta.

case and restored the guarantee to all citizens of equal protection of the laws. One wrinkle was the court's 1955 decision to allow integration of schools to proceed "with all deliberate speed" (349 US 294, 3000), which in Mississippi meant never.

We arrived at a small, rural, white-painted church. The youth of the church sat on the floor at the front, leaving the plain wooden chairs for the parents. It wasn't a church service, but the feeling was much the same. From what I observed, many if not most Mississippi Blacks lived their religion at all times and intertwined it with the civil rights movement.

Retrieved from my distant "memory," this how the event unfolded, though Mel informs me that I'm probably reflecting a stereotype of how well young Jewish men like himself typically know their Old Testament. Maybe my memory alters the truth also because Mel was a much better public speaker than I (or any of my brothers).

"You know the story of Joshua." he said, as I "remember."

"Yes brother," said Pastor Ellison, knowing his flock was in good hands.

Mel likened the struggles of Joshua and the Israelites to those of Black people fighting for their chance, saying they couldn't have a good life without a good education."

"Amen, brother!" said one of the fathers.

Mel probably drew some comparison between Joshua waiting a week outside the gates of Jericho and how long his audience may have been waiting outside the gates of the white schoolhouse. The room was quiet.

"Too long," a mother finally said.

"How long?" he asked in his loudest voice.

"Too long!" thundered parents and children.

Then quietly, "How long?"

"Too long!" It shook the church.

Mel likely continued the story with whatever biblical touches he knew. To get to Jericho, Joshua had to cross the Jordan River. Before *we* get where we're going, we must go to the federal court to get an order allowing *our* young people to enter into the white school house. God told Joshua to march around the City of Jericho for seven days with seven priests carrying rams' horns in front of the Ark of the Covenant. On the seventh day, as God told Joshua to do, he marched seven times around Jericho, the priests blew their ram's horns, and the walls came tumblin' down.

As well as he could, with reassurance from the congregation, Mel amplified in the style of the preachers we'd been hearing all summer, coming round to the basic message, which was both warning and promise of support:

- o If parents went to court with civil rights organizations to win their children's right to a good education, they could very well lose their jobs.

- o But the Constitution of the United States was on the side.

- o God was on their side.

- o And lawyers from the NAACP Legal Defense Fund would be there to speak on their behalf and follow through to see it happen.

A line of parents and children formed to sign up to begin the hard work of integrating the local schools. I vowed to read my Bible more. A teenage girl stood and started to sing. Pastor Ellison lifted his guitar.

> *Shall we gather by the river, the beautiful, beautiful river,*

> *Gather with the saints by the river, that flows by the throne of God?*

On the way back to Jackson, we stopped where another small church had been burned to the ground. It was a pretty spot, nestled in the pines. The church had been about 50-by-75 feet. We walked around the rectangle of ash.

"Who would do this?" I asked, trying to understand what the Klan thought it could gain from burning churches. The simple truth was that the Klan understood that the Mississippi movement was based in Black churches and cared not at all about bombing or burning the down.

Pastor Ellison understood this, and so did his congregation. They loved their own little church as they would love anything beautiful they had created from the ground up. But their faith was in God almighty, who was at the center of their lives every day, not only on Sunday. They'd built the church with their own hands and were willing to rebuild.

Poking around in the ashes I found a misshapen marble of glass that once had been part of a window — clear but streaked by the fire with translucent swirls of brown. There had been no stained glass in this church. I took it as a souvenir.[*]

We couldn't win everything, but we did whatever was needed, even traffic cases. One youthful civil rights worker, "Chico," had been arrested at an accident in Clinton, Mississippi.[†] He was charged with driving without a license, passing on a yellow line and passing at an intersection. He was a kind of fast-talking fellow, a pretty good sign he hadn't been born in Mississippi.

A northern Black youth who would not say "Yes sir" to the arresting officer, he was taken to the local jail and beaten, the policeman saying: "You ain't a Mississippi nigger until you've been beaten over the head."

I interviewed Chico and the witnesses and checked out the accident scene. It turned out that the traffic charges were valid. Chico decided to plead guilty, but he was justifiably concerned about returning to Clinton to pay his fine. I went for him.

Dr. A.E. Wood, justice of the peace in Clinton, was also its mayor. I found him at home, a rather heavy-set gentleman, sitting in an overstuffed chair in front of an air conditioner, smoking a cigar. A copy of *Science* magazine lay on a little, lace-covered table. This told me that, like me, he was a member of the American Association for the Advancement of Science. In fact, Dr. Wood was the head of the chemistry department at Mississippi College in Clinton. It turned out that he had received his Ph.D. in chemistry from Pitt, where my father had been a toxicology instructor in the chem department many years back. As we walked to city hall together, we had a very pleasant conversation about chemistry and other things. At last my chemistry major had paid off. The Mayor helped me get Chico's bail money back expeditiously and I paid Chico's fine. I had never seen such courtesy from an official in Mississippi.

When we weren't getting someone out of jail, we fell back to lower priority problems such as city services. Mississippi towns were obviously segregated and unequal in that respect. White parts had paved streets, street signs, sewers, and utilities such as water,

---

* Of Mel, Gil wrote to Lisa, "I really love that guy. I think I see a lot of what I like about myself in him." Or what Gil aspired to be.

† Most likely Carver "Chico" (later Seku) Neblett from southern Illinois, who left college to work as a SNCC field secretary in many states from 1961 to 1967. Arrested, beaten, tortured, jailed many times, he later became a Black Panther Party organizer. His brother Charles "Chuck" Neblett was also a dedicated, long term SNCC worker and one of the original four SNCC Freedom Singers.

electricity, gas and telephone. In the Black areas some or all of these were missing. I worked on putting together lawsuits to address those inequalities. This was research work, checking out the services in various towns and looking up federal court decisions that might support or detract from our potential cases.

We also worked on desegregating restaurants. Sometimes we defended civil rights workers who had been arrested while seeking service. Ronald Carver was a 19-year-old SNCC worker arrested in the Alderson Café in Olive Branch, DeSoto County, Mississippi Delta.* The charge (obstructing the sidewalk) was somewhat baffling in that Ron had been arrested while sitting at a table inside the restaurant.

Justice of the peace W.P. "Willie" Watkins asked Ron where he was from.

"Originally Boston," answered Ron.

Willie turned red. "Do you know what I would do, if it were up to me?" He repeated the same words more loudly. Ron said nothing.

The JP rose behind his bench. "Well, you'd never get the hell back to Massachusetts. That's for sure."

It occurred to us that this judge might not be completely impartial,† so we filed a petition to have the case removed from the Olive Branch Justice Court to Federal District Court. There were strong legal reasons why the federal removal statutes did not apply to this case, but often removing a case to the federal court resulted in the charges being ignored or dropped. Local Mississippi prosecutors were not usually familiar with the complex removal process and wouldn't respond. Even if we were weak on the removal process the case could linger without decision and eventually be dismissed.

---

*In 1964 right after high school, Ron had joined SNCC. In September he entered the Delta to do voter registration, get Black sharecroppers elected to agricultural boards that allocated acreage for planting cotton, and organize among the high school kids who were the backbone of the movement there. Years later he wrote, "One hot evening in July 1965, I was sitting on the porch of a sharecropper s home, drinking a glass of ice water, listening to stories of his family, work and struggles. I have a crystal-clear memory of that very moment, when I realized I wanted to spend the rest of my life as an organizer. I have done that." After a leading role in the 1968 student strike at Columbia and working in an auto parts plant, he spent most of his career in organized labor.

† According to Mel Leventhal, a Mississippi JP at the time was paid only if he convicted, another circumstance not in our favor.

In Jackson, Prof. Honnold and some of the Lawyers' Committee staff usually went out for lunch, but I usually brought a sandwich to work.

"Why don't you come with us?" he asked. "We've found a little, family-owned restaurant where they serve traditional local food. It's delicious."

"Sure."

We drove a few blocks to a pleasant white business area. The restaurant was modern and looked more like a house than a diner. They had the southern favorites: catfish, fried chicken, greens with bacon, hush puppies, black-eyed peas and fried green tomatoes. Fried green tomatoes sounded a little weird to me and I was not one to experiment so exuberantly. I ordered the fried chicken. It was as Mattie would make it, battered and deep-fried crispy in a cast iron skillet. I was adventuresome enough to try the hush puppies, which were great, kind of like heavy little cornmeal donuts without the sugar.

One of the best things was the service. It seemed like everyone was related, father and mother in the kitchen, daughters waitressing, and a baby sleeping in a corner.

"How y'all doin', professor?" yelled the father from the kitchen as we walked in.

They had just opened a few weeks earlier and it wasn't crowded.

"Great, John, how's it with you?"

"Delicious!" said John. "Have you tried our okra yet? I don't know if a northerner like y'all can take it."

"I'll look at the menu again," Honnold politely demurred.

They knew we were working in the civil rights movement, but that didn't matter. We, like everyone who walked in, were treated like family.

When we were about to leave, Professor Honnold asked June, our waitress, how they would react if we brought some Negro secretaries with us next time. June's face showed some worry but she said, nice as ever, "Let me get Dad to come over."

John came over to the table and Professor Honnold asked his question again.

"We're of Irish descent, so we don't believe in all that goes on 'round here," said John, "We would obey the law, but I worry that they would put us out of business."

"Who do you mean? The Klan?"

"No, our white customers would boycott or just stop coming."

He didn't say, "Y'all come back soon" as we left.

However, we returned about a week later with Pearl and Wilma, our two Black office secretaries. Service was slow. June was crying quietly as she silently handed us menus. The food was great as usual. There were no "events." At the end of the meal we left. Although logically it was a small step forward in the struggle for equality, it didn't feel like a victory to me.

Around 9:30 in the morning on July 2, on instructions from lawyer Mel Friedel, my office mate George Chaffey and I drove to Meridian seeking some notarized plaintiff statements ("affidavits") and answers to questions ("interrogatories") related to the desegregation of restaurants in Meridian. Through something called "affirmative litigation" we didn't need to wait until someone was arrested to get our case into federal court. Our suit asked the judge to order the restaurants to treat Negro customers equally with whites as required by the *Civil Rights Act of 1964.*

Meridian had been the hometown of James Chaney, a young Black civil rights worker. On June 21, 1964 Chaney, Michael Schwerner, and Andrew Goodman, all working for James Farmer's CORE, had gone from Meridian to investigate the burning of the Mt. Zion Church near Philadelphia, Mississippi, in Neshoba County. While attempting to return to Meridian, they were arrested for traffic violations and jailed. Their bodies had been found buried in a dam about two months later.

During the time of the murders and the search for the bodies, Gail Falk, a friend of mine from the youth group at the Unitarian Church in Pittsburgh, was working in Meridian with James Chaney's mother, Mrs. Fannie Lee Chaney, and his little brother Ben. Two weeks after his brother's body was found, Ben Chaney, then age 11, said, "And I want us all to stand up here together and say just one more thing. I want the sheriff to hear this good. We ain't scared no more of Sheriff Rainey!" In summer 1965, George Chaffey made a concerted effort to support Fannie Lee Chaney, Ben and James' sister Barbara Chaney (Dailey) as they carried on the struggle in Neshoba County.

We were practicing nonviolent love, with the notion that you couldn't create a loving and peaceful world through violence. I had read Gandhi, Tolstoy and King. I had no problem with the non-violence, but after a while I was having a problem with the love part.

I gathered that twenty restaurants were being sued, which seemed like a lot for some little town, and was surprised when Meridian turned out to be a fairly large city of about 50,000 with several five- and six-story buildings.

We stopped by the COFO office where I had the honor of meeting Mrs. Chaney and encountered Rev. Killingsworth again. This was a COFO/CORE office, not a COFO/SNCC office. Everyone working in COFO around Meridian was under the guidance of James Farmer's CORE.

Gail was no longer there, but everyone told me how much they loved her. I found out she had become a civil rights reporter for the *Southern Courier,* a small, new movement newspaper founded by the staff of the *Harvard Crimson.*

From the COFO office we went to a Dairy Queen that was one of the defendants in the suit. Being a nationwide chain, Dairy Queen had desegregated since the suit was filed, and we were served without incident. We memorized a long list of interstate products being used or sold there, knowing that a favorite defense of Mississippi lawyers was that the federal government had limited rights. To re-segregate, they would argue that this was a local Dairy Queen and so could not be reached by the power granted by the Constitution to Congress to regulate interstate commerce. The Supreme Court had ruled in the 1964 case of *Katzenbach v. McClung* (379 US 274), that Ollie's Barbecue in Birmingham was subject to the requirements of the *Civil Rights Act of 1964* because it sold products which had crossed state lines. So one of our jobs was to gather evidence that the various restaurants named in the lawsuit were involved in interstate commerce.

From the Dairy Queen we headed for Sadka's Sandwich Shop,[*] a grubby little store in the center of town that sold moonshine as well as hamburgers. It catered to a rather rough white clientele. A few days earlier one of the Sadkas had chased some COFO workers out with a shotgun. Neither was our welcome friendly. Sadka picked up on my northern accent immediately and of course anyone but a regular customer would stand out, especially two boys dressed in suits.

He wanted to know, "Boy, what do you do?"

I told him I was a chemist. He said, "You probably don't know why I asked. You see we've been having some trouble."

I didn't ask what kind of trouble. He continued to interrogate about my name and where I was from. He wasn't impolite, just persistent. He didn't ask George anything. George always faked a thick southern accent.

---

[*] Owned by the Sadka family, children of Lebanese immigrants. The fascinating story of Dewey Sadka can be found online at *meridianstar.com.*

While we waited for our hamburgers, we memorized the interstate products (products that came from other states) in the sandwich shop to prove that Sadka's was subject to the power of Congress. When we got back to the car, we wrote them down.[†]

Jitney Jungle was a chain of grocery stores in Mississippi. The Jitney Jungle stores depended upon Black customers but hired only whites. Leaflets being handed out by civil rights picketers at a Jitney Jungle in Jackson described the issues:

YOU MUST DECIDE:

Jitney Jungle stores should comply with the 1964 Civil Rights Act

The Jitney Jungle stores discriminate against Negroes in Hiring

Uncle Toms, segregationists and Klansmen shop at Jitney Jungle stores.

Whether you buy or not at Jitney Jungle Stores is your decision.

For three days civil rights picketers walked peacefully on the Westland Shopping Center sidewalk carrying signs about the discriminatory hiring practices. On August 8 white agitators attacked and hit the demonstrators. One twelve-year-old Black picketer was beaten by the whites. Another Black picketer was stabbed in the back. Then the police came to arrest the Black demonstrators. Their position was clear: any protester who stepped on Jitney Jungle property was trespassing and would be arrested.

A few days later George Chaffey drove me and attorney Peter Haje[*] to the Jitney Jungle to observe and do what we could. It was a difficult scene for picketing. When we arrived, about twenty-five mostly young Black people were standing around a fair way from the store. Closer to the store was a gathering of whites, some of them looking pretty fit. I decided to join the Black group.

[†] From there, says George, they dashed over to COFO office where Mrs. Chaney and Rev. Killingsworth helped them round up the notarized signatures they needed in time for them to leave well before dark.

[*] A volunteer from New York who continued with the Lawyers' Committee long after that summer. After international law firm practice, Haje was an executive vice-president and general counsel at Time Warner, Inc. Gil and George worked with him also on school desegregation.

Gil's role at Jitney was to observe...

...which meant he couldn't wear a sign.

Photos by Marian Wright Edelman.

By appearance I would guess that most were in high school, but some in grade school. A few parents were there. I could see that the way the little shopping center was laid out you couldn't get anywhere near the store to picket, without being on private property of the shopping center. We were standing on the property of a Negro neighbor living next to the shopping center. She allowed us on her property to picket, but the neighbor's property was really not visible to people going in and out of the Jitney Jungle.

Close to the store was a group of whites, mostly young people, standing around.

One thing I couldn't understand was why anyone would want to shop at a store named Jitney Jungle anyway. The name was almost as bad as the competing Piggly Wiggly grocery stores. But I didn't go in to find out.

Occasionally small groups of Black youth would step up, ready to picket on the shopping center property and ready to be arrested. They did and they were.

At one point, a group of the white youth advanced on the Black youth who were attempting to dissuade Black customers from entering the store. A Black plumber had come to the scene in his plumbing truck. He ran back to his truck and pulled a steel pipe off the rack. Obviously, he had not been trained in nonviolent tactics. Some of the Black youth followed his example to defend themselves. This time the Jackson police intervened on both sides, separating the Black and white crowds. No one was arrested.

With assistance from the Lawyers' Committee, local Black lawyers Carsie Hall, Jack Young and Jess Brown filed suit in Federal District Court to establish the right to picket on private property at the shopping center. I don't recall the outcome, but was a valiant effort that I expected would be hard to win. The Supreme Court had often accepted segregation of private property where there was no governmental action. Also, free speech protections did not apply to private trespass.

The *Civil Rights Act of 1964* (42 USC § 2000) barred discrimination in employment. Claims could be pursued through the Equal Employment Opportunity Commission and then in federal court. But that was slow and didn't help with our defense of the trespass charges. Sometimes you lose in the courts but win in the streets. It's hard to tell exactly why, but America, including Mississippi, is a different place now.

Some who were beaten in events like this or in jail, paid a heavy price. One young man, a teacher, came into our office. He was waiting to see one of the lawyers and getting a drink from the water cooler to take a pain pill, when he collapsed. When he regained consciousness we took him two blocks down the street to the Medical Committee for Human Rights, known as the Medical Committee, He had been having these blackouts, about one a day, for two months, starting when he was hit over the head by a policeman's nightstick. Sometimes the pain was so sharp that he had to counteract it by beating on his shins. He also had been losing the use of his left arm and leg. In those days there was little hope of winning in front of a Mississippi jury, but we brought personal injury damage claims for this young man and others injured in the movement. When the beating was by a governmental employee like a police officer it was "under color of law" and we could file in federal court under 42 USC §1983. *Monroe v. Pape*, 365 US 167 (1961). (The *Monroe* case considered the application of federal civil rights law to constitutional violations by city employees.) Section 1983, as it is called, is a civil rights statute passed as part of the *Civil Rights Act of 1871*. It was also known as the "Ku Klux Klan act."

In later years I have seen many clients with head injuries. Pedestrians hit by cars are a typical example. Usually, the first concussion results in relatively mild symptoms such as headaches and disorientation that last perhaps a few months, then disappear. Multiple head injuries often produce permanent symptoms including severe migraine headaches, disturbed speech and thought patterns, loss of specific skills like math or reading, unpredictable anger and changes in personality from bright and cheerful to gloomy. While it takes extensive tests to diagnose these conditions, and I am not a doctor, I sometimes see these symptoms when I read interviews of heroes of the civil rights movement.

The white racists who beat Black civil rights leaders probably had little understanding of what they were doing. The last thing a white bully should want to face, would be an armed, brain injured freedom fighter, shifting unpredictably from nonviolent tactics to uncontrolled anger.

7. *Speak of the Klan*

On July 17 I chauffeured lawyer Maury "Abe" Abrams to Gulfport (on the Gulf of Mexico) on a COFO matter related to the small town of Newton, 150 miles north of Gulfport. In Newton, COFO was being told to vacate a Freedom House, a wood frame house where a freedom school was housed and from which voter registration activities were being carried out. The fire insurance on the house was being cancelled because there was a fairly high risk that the house would be torched by the Klan. The elderly African-American woman owner could not afford to lose it. The fire insurance was being managed by a white Gulfport real estate agent, whose name I can't remember. Our goal was to get her to tell us the name of the fire insurance company. With that, we could probably get the decision to cancel the fire insurance reversed. Most insurance companies were based in the north and could be embarrassed to be known for opposing the civil rights movement in Mississippi. A tiny pressure could go a long way.

Maury was the smoothest lawyer I had ever met. He was a corporate lawyer, a volunteer from a Philadelphia law firm who deserved the moniker "Philadelphia lawyer."

We met with the agent in her little office in her home. She apparently presumed from Maury's surname that he was Jewish. Anyway, she felt compelled to tell us that a Jewish storekeeper lived in Gulfport, "But he is a true Christian gentleman."

For about two hours Maury talked with her about common interests, for example historic preservation, while he politely turned to the subject of our call, never raising the question of the insurance company name directly, but inching up to the subject in his casual conversation. He approached it from every possible direction until there was nothing for it but to ask directly. The agent said she wasn't at liberty to give that information. Obviously, she was on to us and knew how the company identity could be used. She had politely won the battle to close that freedom house. However, we negotiated a ten-day delay in the cancellation so that COFO could hold a planned rally in the large back yard.

We drove back from Gulfport, through Hattiesburg, toward Jackson, discussing whether to stop on the way. Maury rejected my suggestion that we go a little out of the way to Meridian to eat in a café famous for beating up civil rights workers. I knew that our suits would probably have protected us, as they would never be sure whether we were FBI or not. So I suggested instead we follow up on information from a leaflet invitation I'd got hold of, put out by the Klan.

The leaflet invited us to hear Robert M. Shelton, the Imperial Wizard of the Alabama-based United Klans of America, Inc.,* at a "states rights" rally in Brandon, a small town near Jackson, more or less en route. Also speaking was E.L. McDaniel, whom Shelton had appointed Grand Dragon of Mississippi. Rather than giving a street address, the leaflet said, "Ask any law officer for directions."

Maury decided we had to see it. We drove in, parked and walked into the grassy town square. We stood in the back of a crowd of about 500 whites, most dressed like farmers. The podium was on a platform decorated with Confederate flags. We stood there quietly in our suits while the speakers ranted about outside agitators. I had read the message before, but it was more foreboding to hear it live.

In a thick Mississippi accent, the speaker told us how "The South must rise again." He described how, a century ago, it had been conquered by an enemy that slaughtered its women and children. Now that enemy was invading again and waging a war from within. This was a time of crisis. The battle for freedom and liberty was being fought here in Mississippi. Still possessing a moral fiber, Southerners had come to realize they had to resist the corrupt efforts of the socialist federal government that had no concern for states' rights. Under the US Constitution, each state had the right to govern itself. The Civil War had been about sovereignty, not slavery. The integrationists were attacking the vision of forefathers who had shed their blood to make us free. We had to take pride in that heritage.

One could see how, in Mississippi, hatreds solidified in the Civil War had survived the hundred years since. The state motto was revealing: *virtute et armis* ("by valor and arms"). In small town and rural white areas, guns were prominently and routinely displayed. Blacks also owned guns, but generally kept them out of sight. Rural roadside signs were peppered with bullet holes that brought about some amusing changes. A "DIP AHEAD" sign had been elided by the random gunfire to "DIPHEAD." A former "50 mph" speed limit sign

---

* One of the largest and most violent factions of the Ku Klux Klan, linked to the 16th Street Baptist Church bombing in Birmingham that killed four young girls; the murder of Viola Liuzzo near Selma in 1965, and other murders.

now said "5 mph." A "STOP" sign, blasted with holes that obliterated the "T," said "SOP."

But was the speaker right, at least in part? The stated reason for the Civil War had been, at first, indivisibility of the nation (a need to preserve the union) or, conversely, to enforce states' rights to independence. Later in the war Lincoln, with the Emancipation Proclamation, shifted the wartime purpose to include freeing slaves, but only in the rebel states.

The Klan speaker said that Satan was working through the so-called civil rights movement to turn the children away from God and bring them into servitude to the demonic forces of darkness. The civil rights movement was the Anti-Christ and had innocent blood on its hands.

Obliviously watching and listening, I found it pretty entertaining. Satan was a concept that hadn't been featured in my religious education. Now I was daydreaming that the concept of an anti-Christ might have some applicability to understanding the Klan.

Maury said softly, "Don't look now but there are men circling around the crowd toward us."

I glanced discreetly. Sure enough, two large men were approaching to our right and two more to the left.*

"Walk don't run," I whispered, although there was no need to tell Maury that. We walked nonchalantly, and as fast as we could, back to the car.

The four large men were closing in, two from each side, perhaps ten yards or so away, as we closed the car doors and I pulled out onto the road.

I watched in the rearview mirror as one of the men apparently wrote down our license plate. I saw a pickup truck pull out after us. In Mississippi most pickups had gun racks. In this one, I could see the dark line of the gun.

It was a straight and narrow rural highway with heavy traffic. Passing was pretty much out of the question. We kept to the speed limit, with the pickup truck two cars behind. After ten miles or so, the pickup pulled off and turned back.

"They may have our license plate number, so we'll turn this rental car in for a new one as soon as we reach Jackson," I told Maury.

---

* Gil had been recognized from a previous errand he had run to the Brandon courthouse.

Maury said, "I feel sorry for the businessman who flies into Jackson and rents this car."

For all draft-age men at this time, questions of war and peace had high personal relevance. This was so, whether the young man was inclined to volunteer for the war in Vietnam or, like myself, to resist on grounds of conscience. The issues were immediate, the consequences on the level of life, death, jail or expatriation. For those of us in the civil rights movement the issues of armed self-defense or potential martyrdom were real. In that context I had begun to pay more focused attention to questions of war and peaceful social change.

So far there had been one American Civil War. That states rights rally gave me a pretty good idea of what a second one might be about. How close were we to that? These Southern voices yelling that the South would rise again—was it an empty threat?

At the same time, were we also on the brink of war between Blacks and whites? Next door in Louisiana, the Deacons for Defense had taken up their arms against the Klan. Throughout the South both sides were heavily armed, as is the custom in our country where the right to bear arms finds a basis in the Constitution. Both sides had been trained in military tactics in our various wars.

What kind of provocative act starts wars? John Brown had contributed to the start of the Civil War by his invasion of Virginia in 1859 and his attack on the arsenal at Harpers Ferry. He had believed his attack would be supported by an uprising of slaves, which didn't happen. He was executed for treason, but his death was memorialized in song, and he became a martyr to the more radical elements in the abolitionist cause. After Brown's raid, the South strengthened its militias in fear of similar armed attempts to free the slaves. The fuse had been planted. to be lit by Lincoln's election.

One outcome of the war was the Ku Klux Klan, founded in 1868 by Confederate veterans in Tennessee, claiming, "This is an institution of chivalry, humanity, mercy, and patriotism; embodying in its genius and its principles all that is chivalric in conduct, noble in sentiment, generous in manhood, and patriotic in purpose." Its stated objects included "to succor the suffering and unfortunate, and especially the widows and orphans of Confederate soldiers" and "to protect the states and the people thereof from all invasion from any source whatever."

As Reconstruction included revenge on white southerners, the original Klan turned into a militant guerrilla group intent on restoring white rule in the South and protecting white southern society from northerners and ex-slaves. It soon adopted violent tactics. As part of its resistance to reconstruction, it focused as much on ousting "carpetbaggers" as on keeping the freedmen in their place. This comes through in two questions it put early on to would-be Klansmen:

> "Are you opposed to Black equality both social and political?"

> "Are you in favor of a white man's government in this country?"

Over time, many different secret Klan organizations were established and the FBI infiltrated them to keep watch over their terrorist activities.

Some stories from my own family a hundred or more years ago also reflect the intensity of the feelings generated by slavery and the Civil War that live on in the present. (I'd not yet heard these stories when I went to Mississippi, unless I had heard them from my father as a child. I had a talent when I was young for blocking out what my father said, particularly his dinner table debates with my grandfather about quantum mechanics and his genealogical recitations. I was able to hear them decades later from him on a trip to peaceful family gravesites in northeastern Ohio.)

Back in grade school, I used to think of the Underground Railroad as a single route to freedom. In fact, it was a web of thousands of pathways, a sort of community of ordinary people; and its "stations" had been just ordinary homes, churches and farms, all across the northern states and some in the South. The riskiest part of the Underground Railroad was in the South, where Black conductors did the most dangerous work and were the leaders of their liberation. Whites who worked on the Underground Railroad in the North were principally volunteers, while in the South any whites that participated usually worked for money. It was a criminal activity and so no one asked and few knew where it went beyond the next stop.

On my father's side, my great-grandfather Jacob Tuckerman grew up working in the tannery that his father Isaac had established in 1836 in Orwell, Ohio. Isaac built it on what had been a pristine little stream and what would again, when the tannery was gone, flow beautifully through the tiny town. A tannery stinking of rotting hides was not where most people wanted to go, so later a hideaway under its floor was used to shelter runaway slaves.

Growing up on a farm nearby was my great-grandmother Elizabeth Ellinwood. Her father, John Murphy Ellinwood, was a bad luck farmer but an expert hunter and fed his family largely by that means. His farm included an island on the Grand River that wasn't so easy to get to, but John was an expert boatman. (At age 80 on that raging river he rescued two drowning men.) Under John's stewardship the island became another stop on the Underground Railroad.

Their anti-slavery mission nurtured ties between the Tuckermans and Ellinwoods, and Jacob and Elizabeth fell in love in that dangerous time. They certainly helped their parents in smuggling and feeding the runaway slaves en route from the tannery to the island and northward to freedom in Canada. A poem by Elizabeth attests that *Death is on our track*, and goes on:

> Soon the dust will claim its own;
> Soon our pillow be a stone;
> Soon our mem'ry cease to be;
> Time never stops for such as we.

She was about two years younger than Jacob. Both studied at the Kingsville Academy, an Ohio teacher preparation school. Jacob's best friend in youth was Elizabeth's older brother John. Jacob's first journal entry regarding Elizabeth mentions giving her and her sister a buggy ride. After that it seemed he was always having dinner at the Ellinwood home. They went on to teach in the same schools and to marry in 1849.

Both the Tuckermans and the Ellinwoods left a church that did not actively oppose slavery and joined the anti-slavery Wesleyan Methodist Church. Churches were an integral part of the Underground Railroad, portraying Jesus as the first fugitive because of the flight from death in Bethlehem to Egypt.

Elizabeth's little brother was Ralph Ellinwood, who served in the Union army. His dashing daguerreotype photograph sits in a little gold frame. A sash passes over the brass buttons of his uniform, and epaulets identify him as a lieutenant. He cradles a sword. He has a neatly cropped handlebar mustache. His demeanor is upright and serious, but I am guessing that this was for the photo.

Growing up as he had, Ralph must have been an anti-slavery man, but I wondered whether this was what he was fighting for. After I came home from Jackson, I learned he'd been a professional soldier who volunteered for the United States Army at age 20, two years before the war began. Ralph was captured in an early Civil War battle in Texas. Escaping from an intolerable Confederate prison camp, he made his way through Mexico and Cuba to rejoin the Union Army in New York. His letters to home speak of military tactics: how his greatly skilled sharpshooters with telescopic rifles shot rebels in the head: "The foe dare not show their heads above the parapets or they fall back dead rebels." I think he fought because it was his job and he was good at it.

Ralph Ellinwood was wounded in and died shortly after the battle of Second Manassas, 1862.

As a second lieutenant he was commended for leading his men bravely at Second Manassas, a disastrous campaign in which The North lost at least 30,000 men. Following the battle long rows of wounded (Ralph among them) surrounded every building, awaiting the surgeon's knife. In one field hospital the surgeons dropped so many sawed-off arms and legs out the window that the pile blocked the sun. Ralph refused amputation of his leg and died on September 25, 1862. Only a year before, he had married Rebecca Drake, from a small Ohio town. His son had been born three weeks before his death, but only lived for five days. Rebecca, having lost her husband and child in the same month, lived out her days with her mother.

Ralph Ellinwood's was just one of a million similar stories that, from a southern or northern perspective, entered the collective consciousness, Ralph himself one among hundreds of thousands of men embodied in "Somebody's Darling," a song by the southern poet Maria Ravenal de la Coste and southern songwriter John Hill Hewitt that became extremely popular, north and south: *Somebody's darling, somebody's pride, Who'll tell his Mother where her boy died?* The song is set in a whitewashed hospital ward. A young, dying soldier with no name and no army is carried in to join the dead and dying. For a song this mournful to make the "top of the pops," something drastic had to have changed in the national psyche. Here are two of its many verses.

> *Back from his beautiful purple-veined brow,*
> *Brush off the wandering waves of gold;*
> *Cross his white hands on his broad bosom now,*
> *Somebody's darling is still and cold.*

> *Somebody's warm hand has oft rested there,*
> *Was it a Mother's so soft and white?*
> *Or have the lips of a sister, so fair,*
> *Ever been bathed in their waves of light?*

The death toll of the war was enormous: about 620,000 Americans, exceeding the nation's loss in all its other wars, from the Revolution through the world wars to our latest in Vietnam, Iraq and Afghanistan. The cost continued after the war among the physically and mentally wounded, the alcoholics, and mourners. Hatred has lingered for generations.

In 1965, was a new fuse being lit? The Klan was rising up in general violence against Blacks, Catholics, Jews, and outside agitators. In its view it was fighting to preserve white Christian jobs, white power, and a corresponding "white" way of life. Various Klan organizations were recruiting, burning crosses, conducting murders, bombing and burning churches, and in other ways generating terror throughout the South. The flag over the Mississippi capitol building was literally a battle flag (that of the former Confederate army) enhanced by three stripes of red, white and blue. It had been adopted in 1894 after Reconstruction had been suppressed and southern whites were once again in command of Mississippi. Its staff was topped by a spearhead and a battle axe.

This rapid growth of the Klan coincided with the growth of the civil rights movement and increased use of white volunteers from the North, whose leaders pointed us away from hatred and terrorism. Martin Luther King, Jr. cautioned us not to become bitter. He urged keeping faith with our southern white brothers despite scores of murders, including eventually forty civil rights martyrs whose names are now inscribed on the Civil Rights Memorial of the Southern Poverty Law Center in Montgomery Alabama—men, women, and children, Black and white, "who lost their lives in the struggle for freedom during the modern Civil Rights Movement, 1954 to 1968. The martyrs include activists who were targeted for death because of their civil rights work; random victims of vigilantes determined to halt the movement; and individuals who, in the sacrifice of their own lives, brought new awareness to the struggle."

I want to focus here on the Klan assassins of a few of the many mid-20th-century martyrs in Mississippi and how their cases played out in the state.

Byron De La Beckwith was a fertilizer salesman and Ku Klux Klansman from Greenwood. On June 12, 1963, he hid behind a honeysuckle with a high-powered hunting rifle and shot Medgar Evers in the back. Medgar Evers, the head of the NAACP in Mississippi, was 37 years old and left a widow and three children. In 1964, De La Beckwith was twice tried for murder, both trials ending in mistrials. In following years De La Beckwith boasted at Ku Klux Klan rallies of killing Evers. In a third trial in 1994, Beckwith was convicted of murder. He wore a little Confederate flag on his suit at the trial. In summer 1965 I would find Medgar Evers brother Charles taking Medgar's place.

Cecil Ray Price was a former dairy supplies salesman who had become Deputy Sheriff of Neshoba County, Mississippi. He was also a Klansman. On Sunday, June 21, 1964, in Philadelphia, Mississippi, Deputy Price stopped the CORE station wagon with Chaney, Goodman and Schwerner in it, allegedly for speeding. Deputy Price jailed the three civil rights workers. Price then met with his fellow Klansman to plan the executions. That night he released the three civil rights workers from jail, then picked them up again and drove them to a deserted road. There he delivered them to a mob of Klansmen for the execution.

By October, two of the Klan conspirators, James Jordan and Horace Barnette, had confessed to the FBI, but state authorities didn't bring charges. On December 4, 1964, nineteen Klansmen were arrested and charged by federal authorities with violating the civil rights of Schwerner, Chaney, and Goodman by murdering them. However, Federal District Judge William Cox was infamous for rejecting cases brought to establish civil rights and dismissed the indictments against most of the defendants. The case went up to the United States Supreme Court, which reversed Cox's rulings. Unfortunately, Cox presided again over the resulting trial by jury in 1967, in which seven were found guilty, nine not guilty, with no verdict reached on three. Cox sentenced those found guilty to from three to ten years in prison. He gave Deputy Price a three-year sentence.

Another of the guilty was Sam Bowers the imperial wizard of The White Knights of the Ku Klux Klan of Mississippi. In a May 1964 meeting at a restaurant in Laurel, Mississippi, Bowers announced that Schwerner was "a thorn in the side of everyone living, especially white people" and that he "should be taken care of." Bowers played a lead role in planning the killings and was quoted as saying after the murders, "It was the first time that Christians had planned and carried out the execution of a Jew."

On May 2, 1964, James Ford Seale and four other Natchez area Klansmen abducted two nineteen-year-old Black hitchhikers, Charles Moore and Henry Dee. Seale worked at a lumber plant and as a crop duster. He had worked briefly as a policeman in Louisiana. An FBI informant revealed what had happened. Moore and Dee were taken into the Homochitto National Forest and beaten with bean poles until their bodies were broken and bleeding. Seale duct-taped Moore and Dee's mouths and hands. Then the four Klansmen wrapped them in a plastic tarp and took them to the Mississippi River. They were chained to an old Jeep engine block and railroad track rails and dumped, still alive, in the river.

I made two trips to Natchez (more about these in Chapter 10) before the FBI had instituted any prosecution against Seale or the other Klan murderers. One side of the courtroom where I was working was packed with Klansmen, but at the time I just considered them "normal" Klansmen instead of the cold-blooded murderers some of them probably were.

The federal indictment filed against Seale in 2007, starts, "The White Knights of the Ku Klux Klan operated in the Southern District of Mississippi and elsewhere, and was a secret organization of adult white males who, among other things, targeted for violence African Americans they believed were involved in civil rights activity in order to intimidate and retaliate against such individuals." On June 14, 2007, a federal jury found Ku Klux Klan member James Ford Seale guilty of kidnaping and conspiracy, the sole defendant convicted. He was sentenced to life in prison.

Vernon Dahmer, Sr. was a Black 58-year-old Hattiesburg businessman, a voting-rights activist and a leader in the NAACP. On January 10, 1966, he died as the result of the firebombing of his home. In early morning hours, three carloads of Klansmen had dumped twelve gallons of gasoline into the house and lit it. Vernon Dahmer's house and store were burned to the ground. As he got his rifle to ward off the attackers, his wife gathered their children and lifted them out a window. He stayed behind to defend his home.

In August, 1998, more than thirty years after the event, Mississippi authorities acting under state criminal statutes charged former Ku Klux Klan Imperial Wizard Sam Bowers with ordering Dahmer's murder. Bowers was convicted and received a mandatory life sentence. The other Klan members got off. Bowers had served in the Navy, started college and become a partner in Sambo Amusements, a jukebox and vending machine business. He had also founded and headed The White Knights of the Ku Klux Klan of Mississippi, which in the mid 1960s had an estimated 10,000 members.

On February 27, 1967, Wharlest Jackson, a 36-year-old father of five had finished his shift at Armstrong Rubber Company and was within a few blocks of his home when a bomb planted in his truck detonated, killing him instantly. Wharlest Jackson was the treasurer of the Natchez branch of the NAACP. He had recently received a raise and a promotion at Armstrong Rubber to a position that was regarded as traditionally reserved for whites. The Klan had a strong presence at the plant but no individuals responsible for the bombing were ever identified. The FBI reopened the investigation in 2005 but concluded that anyone connected with the assassination was probably dead by then.

I see some patterns here. There was planning and leadership in most of these killings. Many of the killings involved paramilitary gangs, rather than gunmen acting alone. The Ku Klux Klan was the force behind all of them. The failure of the State of Mississippi to prosecute effectively and the failure of Mississippi juries to convict in the early years is indicative of widespread support for the Klan's actions. This support could be said to be equivalent to that received by John Brown.

These stories of provocative terrorist acts illustrate the potential for even more armed violence, had the Black community reacted in kind as was starting to happen in Louisiana. In the Civil War, many Blacks had enlisted in the northern army to fight for freedom and equality. Why not literally fight again? The reason lies in the non-violent message of men like Dr. Martin Luther King, Jr., and the Christian faith of Black Americans.

In the 1960s I was actively examining alternatives to warfare, but it was hard to consider deeply whether the Civil War had been the best and only solution to slavery, even from a human rights or northern perspective. What had been effects of the Civil War in the decades that followed compared to its lofty goals? Could avoidance of war, even after the opening southern attack on federal Fort Sumter, have led sooner, and with less suffering for Blacks and whites, to the emergence of more equal rights for all?

What would have happened if the North had allowed the South to secede? How long would the southern states have remained slave states? In the mid-19th century, the trend of history was already in the opposite direction.

The abolitionists realized that the first step toward ending slavery would be to end the transatlantic slave trade. By the work of abolitionists worldwide, that trade, though not slavery itself, had been largely abolished by the time of the Civil War.

Denmark had been first to abolish. A 1792 government order ended its small slave trade in 1803. The abolition of the huge British trade was a twenty-year process. Parliament first limited the number of slaves British vessels could carry from Africa, then closed a number of colonies to slave imports, and then in 1807 abolished the trade itself. The United States slave trade, centered in Rhode Island, ended in 1807, the first year Congress could address the question of abolition, as agreed to by the compromise between northern and southern states writing the Constitution in 1787. The Dutch trade was abolished by decree in 1814. The French government abolished slavery itself in French colonies in 1848, having earlier abolished the slave trade.

After 1815, the transatlantic slave trade centered on the expanding sugar and coffee colonies of Brazil and Cuba. British naval ships cruised the African coast to capture illegal slave ships. By the 1820s most slave voyages originated not from Africa, but in the New World. British naval pressure and changing Brazilian attitudes about the slave trade led to government measures which effectively ended the Brazilian trade by the early 1850s. British, Spanish, and US authorities were able to end the direct slave trade from Africa to Cuba by 1867, as slave and sugar prices fell. In 1886, slavery was finally abolished in Cuba by a royal Spanish decree.

Before the Civil War, the Virginia legislature had come within one vote of eliminating slavery. For economic reasons related to industrialization and mechanization, slavery itself was being phased out world-wide before the Civil War. It was becoming cheaper and more productive to hire day laborers than to bear the year-round expense of housing and feeding slaves.

Nonviolent opposition, like the Underground Railroad, which transported an estimated 100,000 slaves, was also having an impact on slavery.

A century later Gandhi achieved a legal end to the caste system in India by nonviolent means. In Gandhian fashion, Bob Moses, Martin Luther King, Jr. and other civil rights leaders and rank-and-file were risking — in some cases giving — their lives. By the '50s they were underway toward many goals of equality without the sacrifice of hundreds of thousands of lives.

In my view, all of the above suggests that civil war may not have been America's best long-term option. However, by 1965, a century of Klan and other white reaction seemed to have set a limit to what non--violence could accomplish. At least that seemed to be the verdict of Stokely Carmichael and other Black veterans of SNCC and COFO who founded or joined the Black Power movement that took shape toward the end of that year.

8. More Talk
on Martin Luther King

Dr. King gave a talk in Jackson that summer.

I was in Steven's Kitchen with two SNCC workers: Antoine, a graduate of Howard University, and Cory, a Mississippi boy from Greenwood, in the heart of the Delta. Thelma had introduced me to Antoine, so they weren't giving me a hard time.

"I hear King is coming to Jackson," said Cory.

"About time," said Antoine. "I thought he had chickened out and moved north."

On June 23, 1963, as part of a national speaking tour, he had lead 125,000 people on a peaceful Freedom Walk in Detroit, Michigan. He and his Southern Christian Leadership Conference (SCLC) were moving their main campaign north. Some read that as a sign that King was abandoning the movement in the Deep South. Was he taking the supposedly easier and safer route in the North?

There, as the December 1964 recipient of the Nobel Peace Prize, he was receiving support from many elected officials. The Klan wasn't much of a factor in the North, but he was confronted by mobs of white racists who threw bricks and rocks and burned the cars of demonstrators. The level of hatred and hostility to civil rights demonstrators in the North was probably higher than in the South. (In an Illinois march in 1966, Rev. King would be struck in the head by a flying brick.)

King had been in Mississippi in 1964 (seen as the deepest of the Deep South, the heart of our darkness, as Nina Simone still sang), campaigning for the Mississippi Freedom Democratic Party, telling its supporters that although they had no money, no guns and very few votes, he saw them as the number one power in the nation. But as of mid-summer 1965 he hadn't returned.

"He ain't chicken," said Cory. "His first stop in Mississippi last year was Greenwood, and we still had Evers' killer, Byron de La Beckwith, walking the streets free."

"Shit." I said, "What was that like?"

"*De-lay* they call him," said Cory, "He walk past me on the street all the time, with a cocky grin on his balding head. Send a chill up my spine."

"Didn't King go to Philadelphia, too, last year?" I asked.

"I have to give him that. He drove right into Neshoba County and walked around knowing that it is still controlled by Sheriff Rainey." Antoine paused. "The problem isn't so much King, as the multitude that idolizes him."

"What pisses me off, everywhere King go, colored folk treat him like Jesus Christ." said Cory. "They brag about having touched the hem of his garment."

"He's just a man." said Antoine. "What do you think, Gil?"

"Well, I see Jesus as a man."

"Are you Jewish then?" asked Antoine.

"No, I'm a Unitarian."

"What's that?"

"Well in Sunday school we studied the teachings of Jesus, but we consider him to be a man, not the son of God. I know King wouldn't like me to say it, but I guess I see Jesus and Martin Luther King as being pretty similar."

"King's a pretty great guy," said Antoine "He's been jailed with us many times. I don't think he's afraid of anything, but he's surrounded by all those ministers in the Southern Christian Leadership Conference, who try to keep him from doing anything controversial."

Whether that last bit was true or not, none of us would have missed King's talk for the world.

Many of Dr. King's talks and sermons were recorded and preserved. His talk in Jackson Mississippi in the summer of 1965 apparently was not. It lives on only in the hearts and minds of those who were jammed into a church near Farish Street to hear him.

King came in tightly surrounded by big ministers. That was the security system in those days. There were no magnetic detectors to catch guns, no explosive-sniffing dogs. It was just a dedicated crowd of men in black, hoping to catch the bullet first.

The crowd went wild in a deafening welcome and stayed wild as King mounted the pulpit. When the cheering died down, half a dozen SNCC guys (obviously not enamored of the cult of personality) stood in the back chanting, "De lawd, de lawd, de lawd."

King's 1965 Jackson talk seemed like an updating of his great "I Have a Dream" speech at the March on Washington held August 28, 1963, the largest civil rights demonstration in history. He began with the need to move from dream to reality. He said that we must use and adopt a proper method. That method was nonviolence. He remained more convinced than ever that violence was impractical as well as immoral. He drew on Jesus' insights, Gandhi's techniques.

He told us that we need not hate; we need not use violence. We could stand up before our most violent opponents and match their capacity to inflict suffering by our capacity to endure suffering. We would conquer physical force with soul force. Do to us what they would, we would still love them.

We would not obey unjust laws. Non-cooperation with evil is a moral obligation. So throw us in jail. We will transform the jails from dungeons of shame to havens of freedom.

He told them to send their Klansmen and drag us out on some wayside and beat us and leave us half dead. As difficult as it would be, we would still love them. They could threaten our children and bomb our homes, and as difficult as it would be, we would still love them.

King promised that our capacity to suffer would ride the Klan down. He said that one day we would win freedom, not only for ourselves. We would so appeal to the Klan's conscience that we would win them their freedom as well.

King reiterated that love is the way. He had seen too much hate. Hate is too great a burden to bear. He had seen hate on the face of Mississippi Sheriff Rainey and of too many sheriffs of the South. He had seen hate in the walk of too many Klansmen. Hate does something to the soul that causes one to lose objectivity. The man who hates can't see or think or walk right.

King talked about how, since the march in 1963, the dream had been turned into a nightmare by Klan violence. Since then, in Mississippi, there had been the Klan murders of James Chaney, Andrew Goodman, and Michael Schwerner near Philadelphia, Mississippi and the murders of Henry Dee and Charles Moore near Natchez.

There was also something new, at least to me, in the breadth of King's concern. He was speaking out against poverty. He said that he had been down to the Mississippi Delta where his dream was shattered as he met hundreds of people living in abject poverty. His concern was not only about Black poverty but as much about white poverty. In Appalachia, he had seen his white brothers along with Negroes living in poverty and again his dream was shattered.

Despite his nightmarish experiences, King promised that he hadn't lost the faith. That he had a dream that one day all of God's children will have food and clothing, education and freedom for their spirits.

He said that he still had a dream that morning that truth will reign supreme and all of God's children will respect the dignity and worth of human personality.

He told us that some day, the morning stars would sing together. We all joined hands and sang,

> *Oh, deep in my heart, I do believe,*
> *We shall overcome someday.*

The ovation was even more deafening than the welcome had been. I looked back and saw the SNCC youth cheering louder than anyone.

In 1966 King returned to Mississippi, adding his momentum to James Meredith's "March Against Fear." I never heard anyone in my life who could inspire like Rev. Martin Luther King, Jr. The cadences of his voice, as it rose and fell, were remarkable. He did not condescend. His thoughts and words were complex. Yet the least educated people in the United States, the African-American people of Mississippi, would carry his words with them and study their meanings, until they understood his message, just as they understood the Bible. I thought I would try to love again.

9. The Delta, Parchman Farm

On July 6, Malcolm Boyd and the Freedom Singers* came to Jackson for a rally. Boyd read Richard Wright's poem, "I Have Seen Black Hands." Wright was a native of Mississippi whose writing was featured in the freedom school curriculum. His novel *Native Son* and other works inspired hundreds of students to see the opportunities of the world, and how to expand them.

Malcolm Boyd read from his own plays and finished with "A Funeral in Harlem," from Ralph Ellison's eloquent novel *Invisible Man*, which had won the National Book Award.

We couldn't afford the movies, but who needed them?† At least I was going on out-of-town "vacations" a lot.

Our "Jewish mama" secretary Mrs. Borden and I drove out to Hattiesburg to file and serve a lawsuit to desegregate the courtroom and city hall restrooms. A 26-year-old Mississippian, Lawrence Guyot (one of the many-times-beaten-arrested founders of SNCC) was a key leader there and statewide chairman of the Mississippi Freedom Democratic Party. Compared to many Black Mississippians, Larry was fairly light-skinned. He was also fairly hefty but athletic and quick on his political feet. He had recently graduated from Tougaloo, a United Church of Christ, historically Negro college near Jackson that was a center for student activism.

In theory, Larry could just pick up the telephone and talk to any of the civil rights lawyers in Jackson. Usually when acting as chair of the MFDP, he talked to Bill Kunstler in New York. But the phones were likely tapped by the local police, which meant that some things probably also got leaked to the Klan. The State of Mississippi had also joined in by establishing a "Sovereignty Commission" to conduct surveillance on the civil rights movement. We took some comfort in our

---

* Boyd was a 32-year-old, white, Episcopal priest and 1961 Freedom Rider. Boyd was also active in the anti-Vietnam War movement. In 1977 he came out as gay and became a spokesman for gay rights. This configuration of the Freedom Singers may have included Chuck Neblett, Chico Neblett's bass-singing brother.

† Gil was getting by on about $25 a week, covering rent, food and other out-of-pocket expenses. He and Willow did double-date once with Jean Dicks and Val Valentine (an out-of-state pair in the Philadelphia Mississippi COFO office that summer) to a showing of "What's New, Pussycat?"

perception that, particularly after the three civil rights workers were murdered, the FBI seemed to be tapping the local police, Klan and us.

In later years, records revealed some basis for our concerns. President Lyndon Johnson was reading transcripts of the tapes of tapped MFDP phone calls and had complained about how long they were. Our suspicions made us cautious about what was said over the phone. We didn't want to something said on the phone to result in a client beaten or dead. Sometimes it was nice to have face-to-face contact for privacy. When we traveled to outlying cities, we law students sometimes acted as that kind of messenger. Nothing dramatic, I don't believe I got any new assignments from Larry, but it helped the lawyers stay in touch with grassroots leadership.

Hattiesburg wasn't in the Delta, but the National Council of Churches Delta Ministry had established offices there and in McComb. The NCC is the major ecumenical movement for Christianity in the United States, supported by about 20 Protestant and Catholic denominations. It provided food and clothing in the poorest areas of Mississippi and worked to bring health care and other governmental services to the Delta. The Delta Ministry also engaged actively in the civil rights movement. The Lawyers' Committee had been called to help steer them in their, so far unsuccessful, efforts to integrate the local courthouse.

After filing the lawsuit and serving copies on the town officials, Mrs. Borden and I met with a group of kids from the Delta Ministry office on Mobile Street. Our lawsuit was playing things low key, not raising the issue of segregated courtroom seating in a high-tension civil rights case, but rather focusing on the ordinary, rather boring, cases heard every day. By this time, the Lawyers' Committee had called the court's attention by simple letter to the applicable law. With that in the background, we and the NCC kids went into the local courtroom "salt-and-pepper style" (to quote Judge Cox) and sat quietly while the court did its business. After a while the local judge went out and had a conference with the city attorney. He returned to announce that, in regard to the misunderstanding about seating in the courtroom a couple days ago, it was now, as in the past, the policy of his court to allow anyone to sit where he chose. He said that he had read *Johnson v. Virginia* (373 US 61, 1963), in which the Supreme Court had stated in no uncertain terms that there was to be no segregation in seating in courtrooms, and would follow it. He tempered his announcement with "unless the order of the courtroom is disturbed or the safety of the spectators is endangered."

Before we left, Mrs. Borden had to use the ladies room. Although she was white, she intended to use the "colored" one. She came back looking confused. All the signs had been removed, not only the "colored" and "white" signs but also the "men" and "women."

Not all resistance to civil rights efforts in Mississippi was of the cross-burning and murder type employed by the KKK. Following 1954 *Brown v. Board of Education* ordering gradual desegregation of schools, businessmen in Mississippi organized Citizen's Councils to use what were then legal tactics to fight integration. The Citizen's Councils spread from the Delta into a "Committee of Public Safety" statewide. The basic purposes were to preserve state sovereignty and white supremacy. They published the names of Blacks who participated in the movement, then blocked them from employment or other economic benefits like bank loans. Legal and economic power lay overwhelmingly in the white community. In this poverty-stricken area there was a huge oversupply of people seeking work.

My next forays outside Jackson involved two cases in the Delta. The first was related to a strike of tenant farmers. The second concerned the arrest of a sharecropper as punishment for an oversight he'd made while attempting to register to vote.

Tenant farming was a system of hard work for starvation pay, akin to (though in some ways even worse than) the sharecropping system that had replaced slave labor after the Civil War. Under either system, in effect, the sharecropper or tenant farmer rented a piece of land from the plantation owner and paid the rent with a percentage of the crop, often 50%. During the year, sharecroppers or tenant farmers would be obliged to get supplies, equipment, fertilizer, seeds, and food from the plantation owner's store on credit. At the end of the farming season they would have to pay for everything along with high interest rates on the credit. It was a rare event if, at the end of the year, they had enough money to pay off their debts at the company store. The only escape from debt was to head north, where conditions were not much better. Many were out of work in the Delta, laid off as the cotton farms mechanized. It was easy for the farmers to find replacements for any sort of striking worker.

Fannie Lou Hamer was an elected leader of the Mississippi Freedom Democratic Party who dedicated herself to supporting the Mississippi Freedom Labor Union. In this enthusiastic time, with thousands of people in Mississippi working for freedom, one goal of the Freedom Schools was to encourage younger Blacks to stay in the South and change the economic system. As Hamer stumped the Delta to gather support for the Mississippi Freedom Democratic Party, she also delivered the message of the Mississippi Freedom Labor Union.

Hamer was a dynamic speaker, a hero to the farm workers, having shared their upbringing, speaking their language, and knowing their needs. The great-granddaughter of a slave, she had grown up in a tar-paper shack and had worked as a sharecropper from the age of six. Largely due to her encouragement, by mid-summer 1965 about a thousand people were on strike in the Mississippi Delta where it was a time to either sing the blues or build a new Jerusalem. For the tenant farmer case, SCLC lawyers Henry Aronson and Chris Clark,* would be up all night researching some of the legal issues, and we'd be leaving early next morning. To have me along as errand boy and to give themselves some rest, they'd enlisted me as driver. With the job of chauffeuring lawyers to the hottest spots in Mississippi, by luck I was a witness stuck in some of the most exciting things going on.

While they did their prep, I sought out Thelma as usual to give me some idea of what I was getting in for. One might suppose, as I did then, that "the Delta" was south of Jackson, where the Mississippi River enters the Gulf of Mexico. But Greenville, where we were heading, was north.

"Just where *is* the Delta?" I wanted to know, and Thelma filled me in. She called it the Godforsaken northwest quarter of Mississippi, black-earth flood plains of the Mississippi and Yazoo rivers. Old cot-

---

* Aronson lawyered for civil rights from 1964-1967 in Alabama and Mississippi, "three of the most fulfilling years of my life." Among other narrow misses: "While on final approach into the small Philadelphia, Mississippi, airport in a rented Cessna 150 with law student Ollie Rosengart as a passenger, we noticed a line of men lying prone on the ground with rifles pointed at us, followed immediately by the sound of *pop, pop, pop*. The only thing that came to mind was to maximally increase speed and altitude and get the hell out of there, which we did, proceeding to a nearby airport. Oddly, once out of range, the only thing we were concerned with was the safety of those picking us up and figuring out ground transportation to Philadelphia. ...No police reports were filed," which would have been pointless in Sheriff Rainey's Neshoba County. Aronson had also been on the scene in the summer of 1964. He reflects, "I doubt that many of us understood the historic magnitude of Freedom Summer. As lawyers we were on the periphery, a small number of itinerant bit players supporting a cast of thousands of stars—mostly local residents and civil rights workers." Christine Philpot Clark was fresh out of Yale law but also married to experienced civil rights lawyer LeRoy Clark.

ton, slavery, sharecropping country. If you see no trees, just mud, you're there. Blacks outnumbered whites two-to-one, but no Black held any public office.

By then I had accepted that Thelma would never get romantically involved with me, but she was always fun to talk to and, what the hell, she didn't seem to resent my trying to change her mind. Besides, she liked to catch up on legal stuff. As a first year law student, I didn't know much, but I was always willing to demonstrate my ignorance. I don't know whether she wanted to keep me out of trouble or get me into it. At least I knew she wanted to see me come out alive. She asked what I was planning to do there, and I mentioned both cases. About the sharecropper attempting to vote, I told her that I understood he was being held on a farm, and I'd be driving there by myself.

"What farm are you talking about? Parchman Farm?" Her look informed me that I'd once again said something lame.

"Yeh, that's it."

"That's no farm. That's the Mississippi State Penitentiary. You'll want to watch your step there. They locked Stokely and Farmer up there for two months."[*]

"For what?"

"Walking into the white waiting room at the Greyhound bus station."

She asked what we were doing to protect the rights of striking tenant farmers.

"Probably not much," I admitted. "They don't have many rights left."

"You mean the Constitution doesn't apply in the Delta?" asked Thelma, with a perplexed look on her face.

"Well, it's still there, but it generally applies to state action. Governments aren't allowed to violate constitutional rights. But the Constitution doesn't usually control the actions of private citizens or companies."

"I guess I heard that before," she said, "when we were picketing on private property at a Piggly Wiggly supermarket. Sometimes it doesn't matter all that much, cause you're goin' to jail anyway."

We also discussed how existing federal law made matters worse for the striking tenant farmers. Since 1935, the *National Labor Relations Act* (also known as the Wagner Act) had been giving most striking workers federal protections. For example, it allowed employees to

---

[*]Also Lawrence Guyot had been imprisoned and tortured there.

bring charges of unfair labor practices against bosses. A refusal of the boss to bargain with the union was an unfair labor practice. The Wagner act also prohibited discrimination against employees who engaged in union activities. Unfortunately, Congress had excluded farm labor from protection under the act.

I asked her how she thought the tenant farming system affected the balance of power between the strikers and plantation owners, for example with regard to evictions.

"There *is no* balance of power," she said.

Aronson and Clark's case centered around twelve tenant farmers on the plantation of C.L. Andrews near Greenville. Not earning enough to feed their families and pay their bills, they had joined the Mississippi Freedom Labor Party and asked Andrews for a raise. He told them to continue at the same rate or leave. The tenant farmers gave Mr. Andrews his key and watch[*] and walked away. Andrews then evicted their families from their homes on the plantation, and the women and children were taken to the Mount Beulah Christian Center, a movement refuge near Jackson.[†]

Andrews got a court injunction limiting the number of picketers to four and bussed in scab field hands ("cotton choppers" who weeded with hoes), and tractor drivers. The strikers had limited success with picketing and trying to convince the new workers to leave. One busload of cotton choppers was turned back in Greenville but another came from Indianola and wouldn't leave. Three of the twelve strikers returned to work but were giving their wages to support the union and the remaining strikers.

The strikers had applied to the Federal Court in Oxford, Mississippi, to strike down the injunction limiting picketing, but federal Judge Claude F. Clayton had ruled that he had no jurisdiction over the dispute. One basis of the ruling was that Congress had exempted farm labor from the protections of the federal *National Labor Relations Act*.

Andrews had then brought a lawsuit against the strikers, claiming that they were violating the injunction limiting picketing and seeking to charge them with contempt of court. There were questions of whether the injunction violated free speech rights of the striking farm

---

[*]Gil may have taken this mention of a watch from a SNCC newsletter from the time. Why a watch was involved is not explained.

[†]The SNCC newsletter adds that the men were taken in overnight by families in Greenville.

workers. The trial was taking place in Greenville, and it was possible that the judge might order the strikers to be jailed.

We left for Greenville at 5:00 a.m. At the trial there later that day, it was exciting to listen to Henry's summary, and some of the Judge's remarks were not what I had come to expect in a Mississippi court:

> "I never thought workers didn't have a right to walk around and protest."

> "We're not talking about civil rights, we're talking about personal rights, a dispute between private parties."

> "It's far better to decide these disputes in the courts than in the streets."

Also, the judge postponed his decision because he wanted to hear the testimony of Rev. Larry Walker of the NCC, who also had been cited for contempt of the injunction. He referred to Rev. Walker as "the shepherd" and said it was quite absurd to try "the sheep" without him.

I would be gone from Mississippi by the time Clayton made his decision, and I never learned the specific result. However, by the end of 1965 the Mississippi Freedom Labor Union was dead. The basic imbalance of economic power had killed it. Economic reality and lack of legal protection for the strikers had doomed this farm labor movement before it had really begun.

My second foray into the Delta was solo. It involved a Delta sharecropper, Sam Echoles, who had gone to the county seat to register to vote. During registration he'd forgotten to put down that he had been convicted of a crime for a fight he had been in some twenty years earlier.[*] For this voter registration error, he had pleaded guilty to perjury and was now imprisoned in the Mississippi State Penitentiary at Parchman Farm. Lawyer's Committee lawyers had filed a petition in Federal District Court seeking his release on bond. Judge Clayton (again) heard the evidence that Mr. Echoles had been denied a free lawyer and had understood neither the elements of the crime of perjury, nor that he had been taking an oath when he signed the voter registration form. Because the state court proceedings to determine these issues might take as long as the prison sentence, Judge Clayton granted bond in the amount of $1,000 for Sam's release. John Doyle

---

[*]A Lawyers' Committee "Report on the Committee Office in the South June 2- August 6" says Echoles' conviction had been for possession of liquor in a dry county.

had arranged for a bail bond, but the bonding company required that property owners sign to back up the bond. My assignment was to get those property owner signatures, as well as Sam's notarized signature, which was also needed for the bond.

On July 14 I drove up alone to and arrived late at night in the small Delta town of Sardis. I had the address of Mr. Carsell Balentine, the only NAACP member in Sardis, but there were no street signs or house numbers in the parts of town that were obviously poor enough for Black people to be living there. But I suspected the town included poor whites as well, and from the outside, I couldn't tell for sure which houses belonged to whom. Driving around the dirt streets, I saw no clues, nor even a light on in any of the houses, nor anyone out on the streets. The only light came from a little clapboard diner painted white, staffed by and serving only whites. I parked, entered, perched at the counter on a red vinyl-topped stool, ordered some pie, and asked for directions to the address I had. They were suspicious, wanting to know why a white boy with a northern accent was looking for an address in the Black neighborhood. But I got the directions and got out.

I woke up Mr. Balentine and got to sleep for an hour or two. In the morning we drove out to a plantation to get information we needed from Sam Echoles' wife. Mrs. Echoles was about forty, thin as a rail but obviously strong. Her simple cotton dress (pretty material with little flowers) most likely had come from a flour sack. Her skin was almost Black from working under the intense sun of the cotton fields. She was delighted to learn that her husband might be released in a day or two.

It was hard to deny the contrast between her life and mine. When I returned Sam to her, it would not be to freedom, but to a lesser form of imprisonment as a sharecropper. She would never send her children to Ivy League colleges. I knew that my parents had, or could borrow, the resources to bail me out of any bad situation I might get myself into. Yet my day was golden. I shared Mrs. Echoles' joy that I would play a small part in bringing her husband back to her. Or so I imagined.

Next we visited Mr. Randall "Son" Burnette, Jr. and Mr. William Burnette, two of Sam's Black neighbors, to get their signatures putting up their property as security that Sam would appear in court as required. They owned small Delta farms, living in multi-room wood shacks black with age. They were willing to risk the little they had for their neighbor.

There were a bunch of little Burnette children gathered around as I got the signatures. One little boy, perhaps three feet tall, came up to me and asked for my business card. I obliged. He took the card and ran his fingers over it. "Not engraved," he said.

From Sardis I headed for Parchman Farm to get Sam's notarized signature for the bond. Parchman was one of the toughest places in the country to do time. I drove up past miles of Delta mud. The 20,000 acres of prison farm were flat and bare, devoid of any place to hide. Parchman had been established as a "reform" measure. The prior system had been one of leasing prisoners to plantation owners who could literally work them to death. Parchman Farm was a prison with no guards, no barbed wire and no fences. It sounds and looked almost idyllic. Instead of guards they had "trustees" who were prisoners themselves, heavily armed. The "trustees" had two jobs, shooting anyone who started to run and administering physical punishment to the other prisoners. The "trustees" were untrained and unrestrained. The law establishing Parchman Farm required that it be entirely supported by prisoner labor, with no additional governmental money. This, rather than rehabilitation, was the purpose of the field work. Parchman was segregated into separate white and Black prisons, and life for the Black prisoners was especially hard.

The Delta blues owed a share of its intensity and power to Parchman Farm. Blues singers famous and obscure studied music there. Leadbelly, Son House and Bukka White all served time at Parchman Farm. Bukka White's "Parchman Farm Blues" was covered by dozens of artists, white and Black. Charley Patton first learned to play guitar from Son House shortly after House was released from Parchman. The story that Patton went down to the crossroads and, in exchange for his soul, learned to play guitar from the devil, is apparently only partly true. Elvis Presley was taken to visit Parchman Farm at age three to see his father, Vernon Presley, who was imprisoned for forgery. Mississippi native Sam Cooke had never served time there, but he'd had a big hit with "Working on the Chain Gang."

As I approached the administration building, I could hear the inmates singing in a distant field. It sounded wonderful, but the call and response work songs were not sung for joy. Rather, they were a means imposed by the prison to keep the work pace as fast as possible. The singing and work ran from dawn to dusk, six days a week.

Usually, when I entered a prison, I would feel a sense of apprehension as steel doors clanged shut behind me. Here the front doors to the low-slung building swung open freely and I walked into a large bare room. Were it not for the armed trustees nearby, I might have thought it a cheap motel.

Parchman's superintendent, Mr. Breazeale, appeared cordial when I told him my business. He said I would have to supply my own notary because their notary was out of town for the day. I asked if there was another notary nearby. He told me that Baron Harpole, the Justice of the Peace of the nearby town of Drew, was one.

I found Judge Harpole at his home on Sage Street. He was a stocky man. He probably appeared older than he was, his face furrowed from the Mississippi sun. I told him I needed to have some papers notarized at the penitentiary and that Superintendent Breazeale had suggested his name. He agreed to come with me. He asked if the prisoner was white or colored. I said he was a Negro. On the drive out to Parchman Farm I told him I was a law student at the University of Pittsburgh, working for a lawyer in Jackson. I didn't mention civil rights because he didn't ask.

He told me about the Pennsylvania boys in his platoon in World War II—how they didn't know the difference between peas and beans. As he explained to me, peas and beans are both legumes, but true peas have tendrils and beans do not. Pea tendrils coil around any available support, allow the plant to climb up to six feet above the ground.

It sounded to me like his sophistication about peas and beans may have come from something more than just farming. I interrupted the peas and beans story to ask, "Did you study botany?"

"Yes," he said, "I had a little botany, before I got caught up in the war." He got back to the story, correcting my ignorance of peas and beans.

Southern peas or black-eyed peas are actually beans. Black-eyed peas have thinner skins than most dried beans so they require less cooking time and don't need to be soaked before cooking. Peas and beans start out life quite differently. When the embryo plant sprouts from a bean, the bean splits in two and climbs out of the ground with the half beans on either side of the stem. The pea, on the other hand, remains below ground on one side of the stem while the stem of the embryo pea climbs up into the daylight. The leaves and many other things differ with peas and beans.

To be truthful, I can't remember all Judge Harpole said about peas and beans, except that the explanation went on for quite a while and, as he told it in his southern drawl, it was interesting. Meanwhile, driving toward Parchman, I was thankful to the boys in his old unit who were helping to bridge the cultural gap between us.

"Do you stay in touch with any of those Pennsylvania boys?" I asked.

"All of the Pennsylvania boys in my platoon were killed in the war." It was almost a whisper, as if his mind and heart were elsewhere.

At the penitentiary we were shown in to see Superintendent Breazeale. Breazeale asked me to wait outside the office while he talked to Judge Harpole. I sensed this wasn't good.

Five or ten minutes later Judge Harpole charged out of the office, his face red and dripping with sweat. He came up close and yelled at me like a drill sergeant. Spit sprayed into my face, but I didn't move an inch backwards.

"You lied to me!" he bellowed. "You told me that Breazeale had asked for me."

Now, *sir* is a word I can't remember using ever in my life, before or after this incident, but at that moment I replied, "I told you that Mr. Breazeale had suggested your name, sir."

"You lied!" Harpole's face got even redder, the veins on his neck stood out.

Again, I said quietly, "I told you that Mr. Breazeale had suggested your name."

"Don't bat your eyes at me, boy!" he screamed in my face. I tried to comply but had difficulty, having had little sleep.

"You little shit maggot! I wouldn't do anything for you even if I had to walk all the way back to Drew."

Drew was about five miles from Parchman Farm and Judge Harpole was not a young man. He had done a big favor for me when he agreed to come out to the penitentiary.

"I would be happy to drive you back."

His war face intensified: "You cockless scumbag! I'll kill you if you don't leave immediately."

I turned and headed out, maintaining my cool and not showing my fear. In fact, I was terrified and believed every word Harpole said.

Leaving was like one of those dreams I have in which my mind is telling my legs to run but they are paralyzed and won't move. Going out the prison door I knew I couldn't run without risking being mistaken for a fleeing prisoner and being shot by one of the trustees. I walked at a fast pace to my rental car and drove away at the speed limit, frequently looking back.

Years later, I now think it possible that Judge Harpole had not intended to kill me, but knew that someone else did. As a justice of the peace, his job was to be fair. I believe there was something about those Pennsylvania boys in his platoon, that he had watched die, that would have made it hard for him to see harm come to me.

I drove past Drew to the COFO house in the Delta town of Ruleville, to feel a little safer before I called back in. I didn't know at the time that this was Fannie Lou Hamer's little town. The brusque, dark-skinned woman who let me into the freedom house could have been she. She didn't give her name at first, seemed wary of a white boy driving a fancy new car, but when I explained she was cool. She showed me bullet holes in the house from drive-by shooters. I called John Doyle in Jackson. Since the notary would be back at the penitentiary the next day, it was decided to get it done then. My presence as a white boy in the COFO house was making their situation a little less secure so I didn't overstay the warm welcome.*

On the drive back to Jackson, not beaten but beat and looking for sympathy, I decided to visit Lisa, working for the CDGM and living very simply with a family in Mileston, a Delta "town" not much more than a crossroads. She was glad to see me, but from her face she seemed to be wrapped up in a worry of her own that she didn't want to talk about.

I didn't want to tell her what was really on my mind either. I had killed a dog on my drive to Mileston. I'd been speeding down an empty highway in the darkness, headlights on but the windshield encrusted with mosquitoes. When I turned on the washers the glass coated over with bloody mud. I could see nothing. A few seconds later I heard and felt a thud. I turned the car back to find a starving hound lying, still alive, in a bloody mess by the road. I stood there

---

* On his return to Jackson at the end of the day, Gil found that his Parchman experience that day had been "greatly overshadowed" by an attack on attorney Barney McHenry, a Lawyer's Committee volunteer on leave that summer from his position as general counsel to *Reader's Digest*. Inside the courthouse in Philadelphia, Neshoba County, after being followed along the halls by notorious Sheriff Rainey and Deputy Price, another man had smashed him in the face with a belt buckle and beaten him all the way out to his car. McHenry stoutly returned to the courthouse steps to press charges, and found Rainey and Price shielding his assailant behind them. "Oh, do you know who did it?" asked Rainey. The face wound required eight stitches, but McHenry elected to drop the charges in this unwinnable case.

watching until it died. Then I felt that I should tell the owner. Across the cotton fields were two lights, about a mile away. Fear stopped me. I got back in the car and continued on my drive to Lisa.

Years later, Lisa wrote what seemed to me like an explanation of what was bothering her when I'd shown up in Mileston:

> "When I was 19, I went to Mississippi as a civil rights worker. It was a profound experience that had a lasting impact on my life. One afternoon I was hanging out with a bunch of local teenaged 'Movement' workers in a dusty community center room. We were just goofing around, and I made a crack about maybe 'fixing' Mississippi by draining the Mississippi River. 'Yeah,' said one young man, 'maybe they'd find my uncle.' 'Or my cousin,' said another. 'Maybe they'd find my neighbor,' said a young girl. There were ten kids in that room, all younger than I. Every single one of them knew personally someone who had been 'disappeared'—who had simply vanished, with no recourse for family and friends, because they were Black. I still remember the dust motes dancing in the light that came in from the window as the stunning reality of being Black in this country in 1965 hit me. The absolute and raw vulnerability of it all shut me up for days afterward."

She wasn't a little girl anymore.

"Come to New Orleans with me for a weekend?" I offered.

"I don't think I can do that," she said, a little sadness in her voice. "It wouldn't be fair to the kids I'm working with."

"It's time," I said. "You've been living in poverty and need a break, and I do, too."

"I'm happy with the beans and rice here. I'm like the others, completely poor. It might hurt them if I went."

"We wouldn't have to spend much. We could take the bus and I think we might be able to stay with Ben Smith and his wife."

"Who's Ben Smith?" she asked.

I told her I thought Ben's wife was a cousin of Gail Falk, our mutual friend from Pittsburgh who had first come down the previous summer. "He's a redneck civil rights lawyer," I added.

She rose to the bait. "How can you call him a redneck if he is a civil rights lawyer?"

I explained I meant that literally. His foot-wide neck was sunburnt red. In fact, he looked like a plantation owner in his off-white suit when I first saw him on the campus at Ole Miss. He was also a huge hulk of a man. The first time I'd heard his thick, Louisiana-native accent, I'd been inclined to keep my distance. I assured her that she'd like him.

Maybe that helped win her consent to go, but not without the caution, "Don't get any fancy ideas."

The next weekend we took the bus down to New Orleans. Ben's wife, Corinne, had asked us to drop by for tea, but hadn't said anything about staying over. They lived in a brick, French Quarter building more than a century old. At another time of year, their wrought iron balconies overlooked the Mardi Gras. They lived on the second story because it was harder to bomb, and Ben represented the longshoremen's union as well as handling civil rights cases.

The danger seemed to come, not from the local citizens of New Orleans, but from the Klan-infected "parishes" (what we'd call "counties") just north of New Orleans. These rural southern Louisiana parishes were the violent areas that James Farmer had described in the spring conference in New York. The Klan stronghold of Bogalusa was about twenty miles north of New Orleans, beyond Lake Pontchartrain.

The "tea" was delightful: Corinne's home-made crepes with a seafood filling and little petit-fours for dessert.

I asked if we could find an inexpensive lodging in the Quarter. She recommended the Cornstalk Inn as beautiful, small, old, inexpensive, and enriched by Harriet Beecher Stowe's having stayed there when she visited the Slave Market in preparation for writing *Uncle Tom's Cabin*.

"That's an exciting book," I said, "I have my great grandmother's copy."

Entertainment was free in New Orleans. We followed a marching jazz band as it played "The Saint James Infirmary."

For a while the mournful melody was carried by the sousaphone, a wrap-around tuba. Nothing could have been more beautiful. It prompted me to tell Lisa my own history with that instrument. In high school I'd wanted to be in the band. I had no band instrument background, and Mr. Zurosky had no sousaphonist, so he assigned me to it. I didn't play it very well, but few people notice when the sousaphone hits a wrong note. On arriving at Cornell, I found I could either be in the band or in mandatory ROTC. I opted for the former and went for an audition. They needed a line of eight sousaphones, and sousaphone players were always in short supply, so I figured I had a chance. The band director asked me for a solo. I explained that I didn't own a tuba, so I hadn't been able to prepare one. He then asked me to sight-read some music.

"Well that's not too bad, but this note is fingered this way." he said. "Why don't you try tapping out these rhythms?" I tried, again with limited success. Finally, he asked, "Can you play *oom-pahs*?"

Those I could play, so I was accepted.

Lisa laughed but didn't seem impressed, so I kept trying, telling her how the sousaphone rank was the most impressive in the band. Only one of us could really play his instrument, but that was all that was needed musically. The rest of us would play the *oom-pahs* and other easy parts. We were there more for looks than for music. All of us would spin the huge silver sousaphones in unison or progressively, bowing or while marching. It wasn't easy, but it was fun.

The player we followed down that New Orleans street wasn't into the fancy spins, but he outplayed the best in the Cornell band. Still, even *he* knew his place. As they swung into the "Basin Street Blues." he dropped back into the rhythm section, playing *oom-pahs*.

In New Orleans we could see the future of the South. The restaurants and bars in the French Quarter were racially mixed. Racial tension seemed to have melted away. People were friendly. Strangers, even of different colors, said "Hi" or "G'morning."

We rode the trolley. The conductor clanged the bells when we got on. Across from us was an Indian woman in a sari with that mysterious red dot on her forehead. Next to her was an elderly Black gentleman whose two grandchildren bounced up and down in front of him. Japanese tourists, loaded with cameras, stared wide-eyed at everything. There was a business commuter, face hidden behind a neatly folded newspaper, seriously intent on looking serious. From the hands we could see he was white. The conductor, a good governmental job, was a young Black man.

We got off at the end of the line, bought a lunch of fruit and cheese at a neighborhood store and ate it in a bright, sunny cemetery. It was not one of the ancient ones but still had a New Orleans feel to it with graves above ground. From a slight rise we could see Lake Pontchartrain. Standing in that beautiful cemetery, my mind did one of its little tricks, falling into some thoughts that I kept to myself. I imagined lynched Black bodies and body parts being carried beneath the surface of the Mississippi and ending up in that vast lake. In this my geography was off. The Mississippi flows past Lake Pontchartrain into the Gulf of Mexico. There the Black bodies probably found their final rest.

By then my relationship with Lisa had progressed to a point where I could hold her hand as we walked back to the Cornstalk Inn. She once had described love in the words of the Percy Sledge song, "When a Man Loves a Woman." I think she meant it as a gentle way of saying that I didn't understand that her life had to be under her control, but with her I felt that I could meet that standard of devotion.

We entered the gate of the famous, cast-iron cornstalk fence which also featured cast iron pumpkin vines. We passed under Corinthian columns at the porch and then walked down a hallway lined with large potted ferns. Lisa's high vaulted room was beautiful. There was a massive old mahogany four-poster bed with a mahogany canopy. The mattress was soft and deep as if it were many mattresses piled one atop another to meet the demands of the princess. The headboard was four or five feet high, carved in intricate designs with a pair of doves near the top. The linens and bedspread were white.

She sat in a chair while I sat on and sank into the bed. I knew she liked "West Side Story." *"There's a place for us. Somewhere a place for us."* I said. Was I sounding like Willow?

"New Orleans has been wonderful," she said. "I had forgotten how it feels to be safe, in a place where people get along with each other."

"Why don't you come over here?" I asked.

She gave her little chuckle. "Don't even think about it."

So, for a week or so, of course I could think of nothing else.

10. *Natchez*

As I'd learned gradually over the summer, as Bogalusa was the Klan capital of Louisiana, so Natchez was of Mississippi,

Through June and July, the *Voting Rights Act of 1965* had continued to work its way through Congress while Mississippi Governor Paul B. Johnson and his legislature scurried to avoid its impact. On July 9, it had been passed by the US House. On August 6, after differences with a Senate version were resolved in conference, US President Lyndon Johnson signed it into law in the presence of Rosa Parks and Martin Luther King, Jr.

The voting rights act suspended literacy tests and other registration barriers and authorized federal supervision of registration in states where such barriers had been in place. It also provided for enforcement in the federal courts and authorized the US Attorney General to send federal examiners to replace local registrars if voting discrimination occurred.

But it wasn't an occasion to dance in the streets. It takes time for momentous, abstract events such as this to filter down into public consciousness and practice. Of course, in our heads we lawyers and law students were dancing, knowing we were headed into battle with a whole new quiver of non-violent arrows. And the act did have immediate impact. Within months of its passage, one quarter of a million new Black voters had been registered across the South, one third by federal examiners. Even in Natchez (a place apart even in Mississippi) real progress was made.

A Civil War city with beautiful antebellum homes on the muddy Mississippi, Natchez was also the home of Klan Grand Dragon E.L. McDaniel.

When it was clear that Congress would pass the bill, Governor Johnson had called a last-ditch special session of the legislature to oppose it or at least counter the provision that would allow the appointment of federal voting officials where discrimination had occurred. More broadly, the governor's amendment to the state constitution would eliminate the complex constitutional voter exam and requirements that a voter be of "good moral character" and be able to define good citizenship. However, voters would still need to pay a $2 state poll tax and prove literacy to qualify to vote; and local voting registrars would remain in charge.

Civil rights marches resulting in 800 arrests did nothing to slow down the Mississippi legislature from approving this amendment, opening the way for statewide voter ratification.

Opposed to the voting rights act of course, the KKK also opposed even Governor Johnson's end-run amendment, but stumping the state the governor used language that most white citizens could understand. "I would prefer," he said, "that our own registrars retain responsibility over qualifications and voting rather than see them swept aside and replaced by federal snoopers in every county of the state."

In the end, Mississippi voters (then almost all white) in most counties approved the amendment two-to-one. Among the half-dozen counties that rejected it was Adams County, where the Natchez is located. This rejection reflected the Klan's hold on Natchez.

So did other recent events. For example, in the previous year, when the FBI had been hunting for the bodies of Chaney, Goodman and Schwerner, a Black leg was found in the Mississippi River near Natchez. Suspecting that the leg had been Chaney's, the FBI had methodically dragged the river and combed its banks upstream from where the leg was found. Finally a chained and weighted Black body *without* a leg was found as well. At first there was elation that Chaney's body had been found, until a second Black body was pulled out of the river at the same spot. Since Goodman and Schwerner were white, these weren't the right bodies. The bodies were so mutilated and decomposed that the only way they were identified was from a community college card in a pocket of one.

The two murdered 19-year-olds were Henry Dee and Charles Moore. The mutilation of the bodies had allowed the leg to float free from the chains that would have held the corpses down below the surface of the river. Dee and Moore had been upstanding young men, with little involvement in civil rights, whose only apparent offense was being Black. They were from Meadville, a tiny town near Natchez. An FBI informant identified several Klansmen as the murderers and revealed that they had been killed because of some Klansman's fantasy that either Dee or Moore was planning an armed rebellion.

In another demonstration of its terrorizing grip on Natchez, in September 1964 the Klan had firebombed the home of Natchez' Mayor John Nosser with an explosion so violent that it shook the Mississippi River Bridge.*

98

In August 1965, George Greene and Charles Evers were leading a march to integrate a public Natchez park with a large, whites-only swimming pool. Charles was dedicated, street savvy, and had worked in the civil rights movement in Philadelphia, Mississippi, long before the three civil rights workers were murdered there.[‡] In an interim, he had been a hustler in Chicago, sending the money south to support the civil rights movement. Evers had been NAACP Field Secretary since 1963 and the Lawyers' Committee had been working with him on various legal problems. We drove out from Jackson to be on hand and found ourselves right behind the KKK's red radio car.

I stood in the beautiful old park with large trees and rolling terrain, a short distance from a line of protesters walking peacefully into the park. The nearby river gave the park a character that set it apart from the usual flatland of Mississippi. Some of the demonstrators had worn bathing suits under their clothes, intent on swimming in the pool, but found it had been drained overnight and surrounded by a padlocked, six-foot, chain-link fence.

Led by Evers and Greene, the demonstrators did win integrated use of the park and, for once, they weren't arrested; but rather than allow the swimming pool to be integrated, the city permanently closed it.[†] I don't think it opened again for decades. What was there about Black and white bodies being linked by water that so offended southern white sensibilities? I think they were afraid that their white youth would see that some Black bodies, like some white bodies, look good.

---

[*] This was actually the third explosion on Mayor Nosser's properties in eleven days. A prominent local grocer and businessman, he had immigrated from Lebanon in 1919. Nosser was a moderate on race, known to say, "When white people get too far out of line, I'm against them. The same with colored people." As a result, he was trusted by neither the Klan nor the general Black community of Natchez, although he employed Blacks in his stores and was willing to negotiate with the NAACP's Field Secretary Charles Evers (older brother of the murdered Medgar Evers). In December 1965, Nosser and Evers jointly announced the settlement of a three-month Black boycott of downtown merchants. At home when the attack occurred, he and his wife escaped alive, and the police rounded up the Klansmen who had done the bombing. Then Nosser's two sons, both loyal Klansmen, had personally put up the bail bond money to get the bombers out. And the epidemic of bombings continued.

[‡] In mid-August, George Chaffey was helping pursue desegregation of the pool in Philadelphia. Swimming pools were serious business. Gil noted at the time that, with the closure of segregated pools for Blacks in Jackson and New Orleans, accidental river and lake drownings had increased greatly.

[†] Philadelphia MS did the same.

The end of public swimming pools, replaced by private clubs for whites.

Photo by Marian Wright Edelman.

However, if any doubt remained in my mind about how deeply the Klan had woven itself into the racist government of the state, it was dispelled about a week later when we returned to Natchez to defend an MFDP worker, Richard Hall, accused of malicious mischief for allegedly kicking a Klan car during the demonstration in the park. To my surprise, the charge against Hall was being *prosecuted* not by the government, but by the Klan itself. Apparently this was a "normal" part of Mississippi law. The Klan had hired its own prosecutor, and the affidavit supporting the charge had been signed by a Klansman in apparent retaliation for police arrests of several Klansmen at the park.

Richard Hall was from New York City, where he edited a company newspaper for AT&T. At the park, he had been assigned the task of guarding the cars of the civil rights demonstrators. On one of those cars three tires had been slashed, presumably by Klansmen. Now Hall stood accused of kicking a red Buick with an antenna on top owned by R.P. Carter.

One witness testified that Hall had been warned by Carter that "I don't want a God Damn one of you to touch my car." Carter's own testimony of what he had said omitted the *God Damn* and added "or even breathe on that car."

Hall testified that he had leaned up against a car but had not kicked it. Charles Evers, who had been called to the scene of the tire slashing, also testified in support of Hall.

The courtroom was packed with Natchez Klansmen on one side and Black and white civil rights activists on the other. The mood was tense, but the judge and police maintained order.

The judge made his decision from the bench: "Every prosecution must be shown beyond a reasonable doubt. There is a doubt in my mind to this extent: Mr. Carter's own testimony was that Hall was leaning backwards against Carter's car. By his own testimony it is inconceivable how this damage could be inflicted 16-18 inches above ground by a kicking backwards motion. If the kick had been forwards, I'd say otherwise. There is no question that on the date in question he was wearing the same shoes he is wearing today and I can't conceive of that damage being done and I acquit."[*]

In 1969 Charles Evers would re-inspire the movement by his election as Mayor of Fayette, the first Black to be elected Mayor in Mississippi since the Reconstruction era.

---

[*] Rick Abel says, "Since that was the first time any Black had been acquitted in a criminal trial in Natchez, the lawyer was carried through the streets in triumph."

11. *Goodbye to Mississippi*

After that second drive to Natchez, the summer project was almost over. I went down Farish Street to Steven's Kitchen to say good bye to Thelma. She wasn't there but Cory and Antoine were.

"Hey guys. I'll be taking off soon."

"It's been cool, man," said Cory. "Don't come back."

I was a little hurt. "Why not, man? You could use my help."

"True," he said, "But you need to keep the good stuff you learned down here and take it to the North. That's where the real problems are now."

"Well, I agree that the slums are worse up North," I said. "The good jobs are taken by the whites. Communities and schools there are segregated in fact. But how can you think our problems there are worse than down here?"

"Down here people live close, they know each other and they let you know what they think," said Antoine, "Up North they lie to your face, saying they like you, then stab you in the back."

Cory nodded. "You can leave 'Sippi to us, we've got thousands of people changing things here. Your job is in the North now."

I thought about some of my neighbors and how hard it would be to change them (especially our proudly self-identified Scottish-American neighbor Mrs. McMahon, but more about her in Chapter 17). "But it's more fun down here," I pleaded.

"So you jus' wanna do what's easiest?" asked Antoine, adding. "You from Pittsburgh?"

"Yeah."

"You've seen the spirit we have here. Take some of it back to that steel town."

"You *know* what's right, ain't you goin' to try?" Cory piled on.

"How many law students are workin' for freedom *there*?" asked Antoine.

"Well I have to go back to finish two more years of law school. It's my way out of the draft," I said, "so I may as well give it a shot."

I changed the subject to Vietnam, where by now the war was raging and, as I mentioned earlier, on the minds of all draft-age men. I figured attitudes in SNCC would be pretty much the same as mine, but I asked Antoine anyway.

"We hate that racist war," he said, "It's hard to move the older groups like SCLC and the NAACP to take a public stand."

"Where does King stand?" I asked.

"We're working on him. You know his heart is in the right place. Since he got the Nobel Peace Prize he seems a little more receptive, but all those fat, old ministers around him in SCLC think that patriotism is a key to winning our battles for equality."

"What do you guys in SNCC do about the draft?" I asked. "I hear that many SNCC workers have dropped out of college to work in the movement."

"Some of the guys just change their names."

I saw Willow before I left, in a more emotional parting than I had expected. She had known all along that I would return to law school in the fall, but somehow she thought that could change. I would miss her, too, but there would be more than a thousand miles between us. There already was a big gap between what she wanted from life and what I wanted.

I told her I was leaving tomorrow by train.

It was a sunny day, but her face was sad. *"No peace shall I find, until you come back and be mine."**

"I'm not likely to be coming back."

"Ooh, ooh, need to hold you once again, my love, feel your warm embrace, my love."

I took her in my arms but said, "Our time is over."

She squeezed against me, *"No matter what you try to say, I'm gonna love you anyway."*

My body said, "Once more," but I knew it wouldn't be right. I wished I had just left, but that would not have been right either. We stood there silently entwined while I tried to think of something to say. Finally, I caught her hands, looked in her eyes and said, "We're from two different worlds."

"You mean Black and white?"

"No. That's nothing. I mean the world of resistance and the world of beauty."

"It's one world," she said.

She had me there, but I couldn't admit it. She got in another last word as I left: "You never know the good thing you got 'til it's gone."

---

* The Supremes, "Come See About Me."

I felt a little better at that—her referring to herself as "the good thing," which she was. She had a sense of self-worth that would see her through.

When I was back in Pittsburgh she sent me a nice picture of herself. I glanced at it, put it back in the envelope and took out the letter. Her handwriting was neat and graceful. She pleaded for me to return. If I would not return, she asked if she could come to Pittsburgh. She said she knew I would need money for law school and she would send me money.

I didn't know how to reply. To me the summer romance was over. I thought I had made that clear. My usual course of action would have been inaction, but it seemed unkind to send no response. I wanted to be as clear as possible. I wrote back telling her not to send money I didn't need. If she did, I'd only spend it on other girl friends.

I took the picture out again for a closer look. It seemed that the dress, actually a sequined gown, was not something Willow would have worn. On looking at my Supremes' albums, I realized the photo was of Mary Wilson, who had escaped from Mississippi to Motown. It was cut out from a magazine. Still, it looked remarkably like Willow.

On the train home I sat next to a college age fellow with a northern accent. He'd stowed a large duffle bag under his seat. In time we discovered that we both had been working in the movement. I asked what was in the bag, but he glanced around nervously and wouldn't say. Only after we crossed the Mason-Dixon Line he felt safe enough to show me its contents: the charred remains of a cross the Klan had burned for him. I showed him the piece of melted glass from the small African-American church. I had to concede that his was the more impressive souvenir.

"In your yard?" I asked.

"Yeah. I came back and it was still smouldering. At first I was afraid, but then I realized that they were the ones who were too afraid to burn their cross when I was home. I never got to find out whether they actually put sheets over their heads, another sign of their fear."

That train ride retraced the imaginary railroad that had run the same direction more than a century before.

North

12. *Pittsburgh & Philly*

I arrived home finding Pittsburgh much the same, myself somewhat different. I had a focus and purpose. I had absorbed something from watching great lawyers bust their asses to help clients with serious problems. I had two more years of law school to complete on a path toward becoming something like them. I knew that most of it would be boring courses on corporations, bills and notes, estates and trusts, and so forth. There would be no courses on removal of civil rights cases, poverty law, corrupt officials, or how to use the law to change the world.

I decided that the Greater Pittsburgh chapter of the ACLU (American Civil Liberties Union) presented the best opportunity for me to remain involved in the movement, so I started to attend meetings of its board and do legal research on issues that came before it.

Lisa went back to Bennington College. On my Honda, I started regularly visiting her family in the evenings, the ostensible purpose being to tutor her younger sister Dianne. Her family made me feel welcome. Stan, the father, was a Russian Jew turned Quaker and an engineer turned ingenious, activist-minded PR man. Alice was an earth mother, always Quaker. Dianne was a year or two younger than Lisa, the next generation of peace activist coming along. Laurie the youngest sister (seven years younger than me), was a budding brilliant artist understandably seeing me as a much older man. As The Lovin' Spoonful warned around that time, *"And then you get distracted by her younger sister."* With Dianne that would have been easy, had I not still been totally hooked on the absent Lisa.

I joined a camping trip to Canada organized by Stan and Alice to take about twenty young people, half from Pittsburgh and half from the little town in Mississippi where Lisa had worked. Even in the summer, the rainy cold climate was hard, particularly on the Mississippi kids. I gave one shivering boy my sweater, which wasn't enough, and thought how tough Canadian winters must have been at first on slaves who'd escaped there to freedom.

We found a small town with a laundromat where we could dry and warm up the sleeping bags and clothes. There, as any bunch of teenagers, we started dancing to a boombox, then formed a line that wove into the adjoining diner. The diners gawked. I guess they had never seen Black and white kids dancing together before. It was generally a joyful trip and I could understand why Lisa seemed more interested in her Mississippi friends than in me. Not long after that, Lisa took a job as a community organizer with a Black gang in North Philadelphia, PA. In time she became the girlfriend of the gang leader, which pretty much sapped my own chances for romance between us.

Young Lisa, Dianne & Laurie Marshall.   Alice & Stan.

Photos courtesy of Dianne Marshall.

After finishing law school I spent the summer in London studying European common law. Graduating first in my class had also given me a good shot at a federal appellate clerkship in the fall. The one I wanted was with Judge William H. Hastie, Chief Judge of the United States Court of Appeals for the Third Circuit, based in Philadelphia. Hastie had been the first Black judge appointed to a federal bench. Apart from Thurgood Marshall, he was the person most frequently mentioned as a first Black candidate for appointment to the United States Supreme Court. Hastie and Marshall were longtime friends, having together won the 1944 Supreme Court case of *Smith v. All-wright* (121 US 649), which established the right of African Americans to vote in southern primary elections. Marshall had once been a student of Hastie, they had worked together at the NAACP, Inc., Fund and on other civil rights causes. Judge Hastie was regarded as the more scholarly of the two, but Thurgood Marshall had earned greater heroic status over several decades culminating in Marshall's victory in *Brown v. Board of Education*. If Judge Hastie had been nominated to the Supreme Court, I would have gone with him as his clerk. However, in June 1967, President Johnson nominated Marshall.

Some weekends I drove home from Philadelphia to Pittsburgh to see a new girlfriend, Nancy. To do so I bought an old Ford V-8 for $100 that had no muffler and screamed like a panther. It dipped steeply to one side, the other side lifted up in the air. It leaned so sharply that you had to pull mightily to the left to keep it on the road. It was always a miracle to make it the three hundred miles west over the mountainous of the Pennsylvania Turnpike. I called it "The Death Mobile."

In Philadelphia I found a church that was pretty much like the small Baptist churches I had attended in Mississippi. It was not the color but the spirit of the church, the music and the sermons, that attracted me most. I was the only white attending and was greeted the same as any guest, asked to stand and introduce myself. Somehow I felt at home.

Getting to church was another matter. I lived alone in the Germantown section of Philadelphia. There were no freeways. I drove over potholed city streets, first through the Inner North Philadelphia slum, then the near northeast Philadelphia slum, then the far northeast Philadelphia slum. All told, North Philadelphia was the largest, most depressing slum I had ever seen. The buildings, mostly disintegrating brick, were old and decrepit. Some were simply gone, empty spaces between two other collapsing structures.

The predominant type of store in many slums is the liquor store, but in Pennsylvania all alcohol other than beer was a monopoly of by the state. So, in North Philly bars were the main type of business. There you could buy a six-pack.

Housing was dilapidated. Factories were abandoned. On Sundays the stores were closed and shuttered behind tall metal grates. In these ghettos Blacks customarily owned few, if any, neighborhood businesses. Young men hung out on the corners, except on Sunday mornings.

Martin Luther King was assassinated on Wednesday, April 4, 1968, in Memphis. The Black community was so enraged at King's assassination that they set fires, rioted, broke windows, looted stores, and stoned police in more than 130 cities in 29 states, resulting in 46 deaths, over 7,000 injuries and 20,000 arrests. Damage to property was estimated at $100 million. In Philadelphia more than 340 people were injured and 774 arrested.

The Sunday following his death, I wanted to be at the church. The only way to get there was to drive a hundred blocks or so through the slums. The trek was never pleasant or relaxed trip, but now I was driving past hundreds of smashed, burnt-out and boarded-up store-fronts. As I expected, the streets were almost vacant, the rioters not up at this early hour. Here and there a torched car still smoked at a curb, but most people on the streets were, like me, wearing their best and headed for church.

The morning service was subdued. There was no particular wel-come for me, but I presumed that was because I had become a regular, and not a guest. Apart from a few words said for King, the sermon was much the same as usual.

It had not occurred to me that, when church ended at noon and people were generally awake and about, the risks for a white boy driv-ing back toward Germantown would be greater, but I drove back without trouble through block after block of destruction.

I try not to think about the death of the Rev. Martin Luther King, Jr. His lessons, as preserved in his speeches, autobiography and other writings did not die with him, but to me the movement itself seemed to fade.

When I do still recall his death, the song that comes to mind is nothing like the hopeful songs we'd sung. Kate McGarrigle's "Heart Like a Wheel" had yet to be written, but for me, the emotions are linked:

> *And it's only love, and it's only love,*
> *That can wreck a human being and turn him inside out.*
> *But my only wish is for that deep dark abyss,*
> *'Cause what's the use of living with no true lover.*

13. The ACLU & Pittsburgh's Tactical Police

At the end of my one-year clerkship I was offered what seemed like my ideal job. Tom Kerr was President of the Pennsylvania chapter of the American Civil Liberties Union. Through it, he somehow combined vigorous defense of the constitution with salaried corporate antitrust law for Westinghouse and the teaching of law. We knew each other well already through his having had me as a teenager in Sunday school, and through the research I'd already done as an ACLU volunteer.[*]

"Would you consider coming to work for the Greater Pittsburgh ACLU as our first Executive Director?" he asked. By "Greater Pittsburgh" he meant all of Western Pennsylvania.

I said I would because it would allow me to bring my Mississippi experience north.

"That's what we're looking for," he said. "If we could bring the prejudices out in the open, they would be easier to fight."

"Could I live on the pay?"

"I think I could promise you half the salary of the large downtown firms. But you'll be able to live comfortably—if you can raise the money."

"How about the hours?"

"Don't worry, there will be enough. Like in Mississippi, you'll only be working when there are problems. And you'll be able to spread your time into the nights if the days get slow."

This was good because it would afford me the time to also pursue a Pitt master's degree in public health.

"What about staff?"

"You'll have Marian Damick part time to answer the phones. Better yet, you'll have a 'staff'!"

By that he meant the aid of a hundred volunteer attorneys in Pittsburgh's Allegheny County plus another twenty from outlying counties.

---

[*] "A role model for many of us, willing to stand up for equal rights and equal opportunity for everyone. He believed it was the duty of the government to protect and promote those objectives." —Michael Louik, Pennsylvania ACLU state president, 2006.

I could personally handle the crisis cases. Other cases I could take myself or farm out to the more experienced volunteer lawyers, or team up on them if I chose. Less experienced lawyers I'd need to help and manage closely.

For me, that clinched the deal. To have Tom Kerr, a giant of the legal community, working *for* me (not to mention the other experienced volunteers) was more than any young lawyer could want. I had many mentors in the ACLU. It was the land and time of mentors, the greatest being Tom Kerr. There were half a dozen law professors in the group plus two university presidents who didn't need to be lawyers to be great assets. The organization was founded on the wisdom of mentors like James Madison, Thomas Jefferson, Benjamin Franklin and George Washington. Everyone in the ACLU was dedicated to helping me implement those values that had been enshrined in the Bill of Rights. Well, perhaps one member wasn't so dedicated. Abbie Hoffman helped me spot him.

Abbie was one of the Chicago Seven: targets of a roundup of originally eight radical leaders charged with conspiring to disrupt the 1968 Democratic Party convention in Chicago. Bill Kunstler, both lawyer and one of the world's greatest stand-up comedians, turned their courtroom defense into a searing attack on US policies in Vietnam. Abbie and I both spoke at a conference at the University of Pittsburgh on the subject of political oppression. There he talked about how to spot the FBI informant in a group: it was always the guy in the windbreaker jacket.

Well, that opened my eyes a bit, since we had one ACLU board member who always wore a windbreaker jacket. I figured the ACLU wasn't important enough or radical enough to have its very own FBI informant, but this guy was active in all of the most leftist groups in town. He was always mouthing off the most radical opinions imaginable. Before I'd left for Mississippi, he'd hinted that he really wasn't as radical as he pretended. As one of my professors, he'd taken me aside and warned me not to associate with certain "communist" groups in Mississippi, even though these were groups to which he said he belonged. In the military he had served in internal security. He repeatedly volunteered to take over the work of managing the ACLU membership list; I kept putting him off with flimsy excuses.

My general choice in life has been to trust everyone to be who they claim to be (of course, eyes open for windbreaker jackets). The price may be occasional betrayal, but I prefer to have a spirit free of distrust.

Headquartered in Pittsburgh, the United Steelworkers (USW, the country's largest industrial union) was relatively proactive in permitting membership of Blacks, but the plumbers, carpenters and other trade unions were white enclaves, where membership was typically passed down from a member to his son or other close relative. The USW represented industrial workers in many industries, not only steel. The problem for Blacks there was getting promoted. The problem in the other unions was that they didn't hire Blacks in the first place.

One of the most significant civil rights movements in Pittsburgh was the Black Construction Coalition (BCC), which struggled to integrate the construction industry work force. The drama would be played out at the massive Steelers' and Pirates' Three Rivers Stadium, one of the most economically important construction settings in the Pittsburgh area. It would be the scene for repeated attacks by the Pittsburgh Tactical Police Force (TPF) on protesters from the BCC.

Ground was broken for the stadium project on April 25, 1968. I fell into the thick of the legal defense when I arrived in Pittsburgh a few weeks later. Blacks were shut out of the hiring process there and on other public works construction contracts because all hiring was done through the craft unions, in which only two Blacks had been accepted as members.

The TPF looked like an old-fashioned version of Star Wars storm troopers. A step before their time, they wore dark plastic armor from head to toe. Their helmets might have passed for clunky versions of modern skateboard helmets. They brandished super-sized nightsticks; for some reason the normal size would not suffice. They moved together carrying shields like a Roman legionnaires.

They didn't have an easy job. Over the potholed Pittsburgh streets, they rode jammed together, inside a hot, dark, windowless truck, unable to see where they were going. Occasionally some were sick from the ride. On arrival the rear door was thrown open and they rushed out into the blinding light, prepared to attack whatever was there.

As construction proceeded, multiple ramps curved up the side of rising stadium, one level over another. This provided a dramatic setting for the maneuvers of the TPF. Hundreds of members of the Black Construction Coalition were confronting the trade unionists who felt they owned an exclusive right to employment on public jobs. The TPF supported the unions by beating and arresting Black job applicants.

In the confrontations, the Black potential construction workers sometimes offered more than passive resistance. Under my direction, the ACLU represented 100 or more of the arrested Black coalition picketers, with mixed success.

Tom Kerr, 1983. *ACLU photo.*

Nate Smith around 1969. *Photo by Harry Coughanour, Pittsburgh Post-Gazette.*

The BCC was led by Nate Smith, one of Pittsburgh's most dynamic civil rights leaders. Nate was not afraid to lie down in front of bulldozers to stop work at construction sites. But he also formed a creative job training program. He'd enlisted in the US Navy at age twelve and learned how to operate heavy machinery before his age was discovered and he was booted out. With what he'd learned back then, he launched Operation Dig in 1969. He took out loans on his home to help pay for heavy equipment for the program. Within two years he had trained and qualified ninety African Americans to be card-holding union members working on various job sites in Western Pennsylvania. To actually get them hired, the BCC stopped work on ten building projects, including the stadium site. Smith's strategy relied on a contractor's view of delays. "Contractors don't like that," he said. "When a site shuts down, they lose a lot of money, so they listened to me, and they hired Blacks."

The Black Construction Coalition didn't end all discrimination in employment against Blacks in Pittsburgh. That would remain a long term job for the ACLU, the Urban League, the NAACP and the Equal

Employment Opportunity Commission. But the BCC had opened jobs for Blacks in the hardest industry in town.

The Pittsburgh Tactical Police Force continued its work of responding to demonstrations the only way it knew how. Rather than just sitting in the station doing nothing, it set out against targets including the United Farm Workers of America. UFW leader Cesar Chavez sent representatives across the country to organize a grape boycott. To Pittsburgh he sent Al Rojas, and soon the major supermarkets in Pittsburgh were participating in the boycott. Pittsburgh was generally a union town, where people were not accustomed to crossing picket lines. Only some small independent grocers persisted in selling grapes.

I defended eleven persons arrested at a grape boycott protest at a downtown fruit stand, including one priest and four nuns, all charged in magistrate court with disorderly conduct. The arresting officer testified that he arrested everyone because they had continued to demonstrate even after the store had stopped selling grapes. However, the owner admitted that he was still selling grapes and only stopped temporarily when the picketers appeared. I said that none of that mattered. All that mattered was the free speech rights of American citizens. City of Pittsburgh Magistrate Troiano dismissed all charges.

The TPF was then deployed against the boycott leaders and demonstrators. This seemed like overkill to me, inasmuch as Al Rojas, though large in spirit, was physically one of the tiniest union organizers ever to arrive in Pittsburgh. The tactical patrol arrested grape boycott demonstrators in the "Strip" district of town, where produce came in by the truckload and was sold wholesale to the supermarkets and restaurants. For talking to a truck driver, the demonstrators were charged with obstructing traffic and beaten by the TPF. We appealed their convictions.

The most blatant illegal use of police force during my time with the Pittsburgh ACLU occurred in a magistrate's courtroom. A group of draft resistors had been arrested and charged with disorderly conduct for demonstrating at a draft board member's home on March 18, 1970. I sent two of my best volunteer attorneys, Michael Louik (my high school classmate and friend) and Harry Swanger, to defend them. In the courtroom, a police officer violently pulled the long pony-tail hair of one of the defendants. Some in the crowd rose to protest. The magistrate, Robert Dauer, ordered the courtroom to be cleared. The police moved everyone out to the adjoining anteroom. Then all the lights went out and the TPF piled into the demonstrators and court-room spectators, beating them with clubs.

Several of the demonstrators suffered head injuries in the melée. After the incident some of the police lodged complaints that their right hands had been injured. This was presumably caused by demonstrators using their heads to hit the police on the hand. It seemed to follow a pattern that whenever the police beat someone up, that person was charged with assault on an officer.

Five of those who were beaten up were arrested and charged for their alleged acts in the police ambush. They became known as the Pittsburgh Five. One of them was Paul Boas, a handsome and articulate law student with long sideburn and later a prominent defense lawyer himself. I think it was Paul who called Bill Kunstler in New York. Kunstler answered his own phone and immediately offered to help.

By that time Kunstler was famous for his successful defense of the Chicago Seven. He was a shaggier, more radical man than I had known in Mississippi, but no less brilliant and no less charming. On behalf of his clients, he said things to judges that other lawyers were afraid to say. This had earned him 24 citations for contempt of court, and four-year-plus prison sentence from Judge Julius Hoffman in the Chicago Seven trial. But Kunstler had gone to the edge of propriety and not over it, and all of the contempt citations were reversed on appeal.

Kunstler came down to Pittsburgh and teamed up with Michael Louik and Harry Swanger. He reached into his bag of tricks and pulled out the 1965 case of *Dombrowski v. Pfister* (380 US 479). Bill had been one of the lawyers who took that famous civil rights case to the United States Supreme Court, back when I first knew him. In *Dombrowski*, the Supreme Court had ordered that a Louisiana state criminal prosecution of leaders of the Southern Conference Educational Fund, a civil rights organization, not be allowed to proceed, that papers seized from them had to be returned to them, and that a Louisiana law requiring them to register as communists be regarded as void. The *Dombrowski* case was unusual in that it was the more common practice for the federal courts to allow the state courts to proceed with criminal prosecutions, reversing unconstitutional actions only after the state proceedings were over.

This also was a pretty unusual situation, in which Americans had engaged in an expression of free speech, then had been beaten up in a courtroom without even first getting a trial, then charged with assaulting the police. It seemed a bit like the Queen of Hearts in *Alice in Wonderland*, who decreed that the sentence should come before the trial.

No one else in the world could present such a case more passionately and articulately than Bill. He and the other lawyers filed a *"Dombrowski"* action in federal court asking it to stop the state court prosecutions. Kunstler argued that Pennsylvania's prosecution of the draft protesters was done in bad faith and was designed to chill and deter First Amendment expression. I'm not sure by what procedures exactly, but the major charges against all of the Pittsburgh Five were dismissed, three pled guilty to minor charges and two were acquitted at trial. Paul Boas' charges were all dismissed.

In the end we won the war with the Pittsburgh Tactical Police Force. Peter Flaherty had been elected mayor of Pittsburgh in 1969. He eliminated the unit because of its role in suppressing the rights of African Americans.

14. Feminists & Weatherwomen

I once asked my father how feminism had affected his life. My perception at the time was that my parents' marriage had been very conventional: he working full time, she taking care of the kitchen and household.

His answer surprised me. He said the feminist movement had not affected him at all because all the women in his family were feminists. I was skeptical until he told me their stories.

The connection is clearest on my Tuckerman side, but I should mention that on my Venable side great-grandmother Mary Vater Venable had a renegade upbringing and obtained a good education in an interesting way. Political refugees from England, her parents joined a communal society in an Ohio town called Utopia. Since Utopia had no school or teacher, as a girl Mary Vater sat many hours under an old oak overlooking the Ohio River, reading the classics of her day. (I drove through Utopia once. The old communal buildings were still standing, vacant, grey with age.) Advancing to young womanhood in the Midwest, Mary hung out with a literary circle. Her best friend Fanny was a magazine fiction writer who married Robert Louis Stevenson, the most popular author in the world at that time. In those days a degree was not required to become a teacher, and Mary went into that profession before marrying another non-degreed teacher, my great-grandfather Hal Venable, whose ramble "Down South..." I summarized in Chapter 2. Eventually, their son William Mayo Venable (my grandfather) would marry a Tuckerman daughter.

In their generation, all women on both the Venable and Tuckerman sides went on to college and related careers.

Both families were big on books. The library of my great-grandmother Elizabeth Ellinwood Tuckerman included *The Wrongs of Woman* by Charlotte Elizabeth Tonna, published in 1844. The title plays on the fact that at that time women had virtually no legal *rights*: in this country: very limited rights to own property, no right to divorce, no right to custody of their children, no right to hold public office, no right to serve as jurors. In no advanced society anywhere did they have the right to vote. Meanwhile the industrial revolution had stripped many women of home and family support. Instead of the domestic life they theoretically enjoyed, many were indentured to work in factories and lived in urban poverty.

Great-grandfather Jacob Tuckerman had attended Oberlin College for three years starting in 1847. Oberlin was the first American college to grant degrees to women and to accept students of all races. One of Jacob's classmates at Oberlin had been Lucy Stone, a suffragist and abolitionist. Another Oberliner at that time was Antoinette Louisa Brown, who in 1853 became the first ordained woman minister in the United States.

Oberlin's experiment with educating men and women together chilled many contemporaries with a specter of breakdown in sexual morals. Oberlin was also a center of abolitionism, a station on the Underground Railroad. Shockingly in 1835, it began to admit Black students alongside white.

Jacob and Elizabeth saw to it that both their sons and daughters could attend college. Jacob also sold his property in Orwell in order to send his daughter Florence Tuckerman for post graduate study of the classics in Greece, enabling her to teach the classics at a college level for many years. Florence's sister, my grandmother (Jessie Tuckerman Venable) and other Tuckerman women graduated from Oberlin. Jessie became one of the country's first settlement house social workers and, only in her mid-thirties, stepped down as head of social work at the Cincinnati Social Settlement to marry.

The feminist star of that generation was Jacob and Elizabeth Tuckerman's granddaughter, Florence Ellinwood Allen[*] (born in 1884), who would set more firsts for women in the legal system than anyone else in history.

The daughter of an academic, by age eight Florence Ellinwood Allen knew Latin and Greek. Her early career aim was in music, but an injury rerouted her into law. In 1912, a year before graduating second in her class at NYU Law School (which she financed by working for The New York League for the Protection of Immigrants), she joined an Ohio referendum effort in support of women's suffrage. Though the turnout for her campaign talks was sometimes small, she gave 92 of them across Ohio's 88 counties and learned a lot about dealing with hecklers. The state referendum effort lost, but Ohio women would gain the right to vote in 1920 with the passage of the Nineteenth Amendment.

In 1916, Florence persuaded the Ohio Supreme Court to uphold local ordinances granting women the right to vote in several municipal

---

[*] Not to be confused with Jessie Tuckerman's scholarly sister Florence Tuckerman. It was a popular 19th-century name.

elections. In 1919, she became the first female appointment to a county prosecutor's staff. In 1920, she won a race against nine male opponents to become America's first general trial court judge. She credited the women's movement for the victory.

At first, the other judges typecast Judge Allen, asking her to handle family court proceedings, but she insisted on handling the same work as they. As she later remembered, "I didn't see why I should sit on the Domestic Relations Bench, when I am an old maid, and there are many fathers on the Bench."

Judge Allen was the first woman to preside over a murder trial with women sitting on the jury. She was the first woman to sentence a man to death, a difficult decision for her. In 1922, the voters of Ohio elected her the first woman in the United States to sit on a state supreme court. She took office despite the claims of some that women had no right to hold office but only the right to vote. This victory made her "the most famous woman judge in the world."

When Florence first arrived for a meeting with her all-male colleagues on the Supreme Court of Ohio, she sensed a certain uneasiness among them. Florence was perceptive enough to identify the cause of their discomfort and told them that, although she herself did not smoke, they should feel free to do so themselves. The tensions then quickly diminished, as the males took out their pipes and cigars. Her election secured a liberal majority on the court, and she voted for a number of progressive causes, including workers' rights and peaceful picketing.

In 1934, by nomination of President Franklin Roosevelt and unanimous confirmation by the Senate, she became the first woman to serve on a United States Circuit Court of Appeals. In 1938, Judge Allen wrote one of her most important decisions, upholding the Tennessee Valley Authority, an important piece of FDR's New Deal legislation. In 1959, she became the first woman to be chief judge of a federal circuit court. During much of the 1930s and '40s, she was the only woman serving as a federal judge.

In her book *This Constitution of Ours*, she wrote, "Liberty cannot be caged into a charter and handed on ready-made to the next generation. Each generation must recreate liberty for its own times. Here in America we inherited an instrument apt for shaping freedom. Whether or not we establish freedom rests with ourselves."

Florence Ellinwood Allen.

I had to admit that my father's ancestral kin were strong, feminist women. But, in accordance with a strong, stubborn streak among the men in my family, I didn't have to admit that my father was a feminist.

I didn't know about Florence when I decided to go to law school. I thought I was blazing a path new to my family. But I later framed her robed photo portrait and hung it in my offices. I liked to look closely at her hands: rough and crusted with dirt because she loved to garden.

By the late '60s, the cause of feminism looked a little different than it had around 1920. More equalities in rights were gaining recognition. In Pittsburgh the National Organization for Women (NOW) filed a complaint with the city Human Relations Commission. The goal was to eliminate columns of ads titled "Help Wanted Male" and "Help Wanted Female." Conflicting rights were claimed in the case inasmuch as the *Pittsburgh Press* claimed that its right to discriminate against women was based on the rights of freedom of speech and freedom of the press.

Marjorie Matson represented NOW. Marjorie was a 1932 graduate of Pitt's College of Law and was the first woman hired to serve as a prosecuting attorney in the Pittsburgh area. At the time of NOW's HRC complaint, she was an experienced lawyer in private practice and also served as President of the local chapter of the ACLU.

The city Human Rights Commission was represented by Marian Finkelhor, an attorney in the city's law department. Marian's husband, Howard, had been a friend of my father since kindergarten. When Marian ran for a superior court judgeship, my mother was her campaign manager. As such, she recruited her friends in the Parent Teacher Associations, Den Mothers in the Cub Scouts, Cornell Women's Club members, and women from other organizations to help get Marian elected. Becoming a judge forced Marian to discontinue representing the Human Rights Commission, but Eugene Strassburger replaced her.

I filed an *amicus curiae* (friend of the court) brief at the start of the case in the Pittsburgh Human Relations Commission for the Pittsburgh ACLU challenging the sex-segregated help-wanted listings in the *Pittsburgh Press*. An amicus brief can only be filed with the permission of the court or commission. It differs from the briefs filed by the parties in that the judges don't have to read it. The goal was to eliminate separate columns titled "Help Wanted Male" and "Help Wanted Female," but the case raised claims of conflicting rights. The *Pittsburgh Press* based its claim to the right to gender-segregate the employment ads on the rights of freedom of speech and freedom of the press. We won in the Commonwealth Court, sustaining the decision by the Pittsburgh Human Relations Commission. Unfortunately, the *Pittsburgh Press* got a stay of the order from the Pennsylvania Supreme Court, pending appeal. The issue finally was settled in 1973 in *Pittsburgh Press v. Pittsburgh Commission on Human Relations* (413 US 376).

At the Supreme Court level, writing the amicus brief for the ACLU, which I had done at the initial stage of the case, was taken on by the national office of the ACLU and its Women's Rights Project, co-founded and headed by Professor (and future Supreme Court Justice) Ruth Bader Ginsburg. Organizations which file amicus briefs, not representing a party to the case, are not generally allowed to participate in oral argument before the Supreme Court.

A question arose about whether Ginsburg or Matson should be handed the great honor of arguing the case at that level. The national ACLU office wanted Ginsburg to do it. But Marjorie Matson didn't give up. She'd been selected by NOW to argue the case and, as client, NOW was entitled to important decisions. In the end, Matson and Gene Strassburger of the City of Pittsburgh Law Department equally split the time for oral argument. Both did magnificent jobs.

In a five-four decision, the court held that employers' and newspapers' use of sex-segregated "Male Help Wanted" and "Female Help Wanted" columns was illegal, because it enabled employers to express unlawful gender preferences. The newspaper's First Amendment rights did not extend to discriminatory commercial speech.

This decision was the first Supreme Court ruling that discrimination on the basis of sex is a "suspect category" under the equal protection clause. It also spelled out new concepts related to commercial speech (advertisements) being more susceptible to regulation than are political forms of free speech. It is one of the most frequently cited decisions of the Supreme Court.

Another burning women's rights issue was abortion. In 1967 the ACLU's national board had affirmed a woman's constitutional right to abortion and called for the repeal of all criminal abortion laws. But the local chapters of ACLU were free to take their own positions. The Greater Pittsburgh ACLU sponsored a debate "Abortion and the Constitution." The issue hadn't then reached the Supreme Court, but positions like those of the ACLU could be a major influence on future Court decisions. The issues presented for the debate in Pittsburgh were listed as "due process," "free speech" and "equal protection of the laws." Yet these all miss the central constitutional issue as seen by the Supreme Court in 1983 in its eventual opinion in *Roe v. Wade* (410 US 113).

Roe v. Wade was decided primarily on the Ninth Amendment. The amendment says in part, "the enumeration in the Constitution, of certain rights, shall not be construed to deny or disparage others retained by the people," and the court decided that this included a person's right to privacy. Of course, you can't find the actual phrase "right to privacy" anywhere in the Bill of Rights as written by the founding fathers. The Supreme Court had to look for it in the "penumbra" of the Ninth Amendment. Penumbras are hard places for literal people to find, so there was plenty of room for debate between those who read the Constitution literally and those who sought its spirit.

In 1969, the "weatherwomen" (members of a group that initially called itself the Women's Brigade of the Weather Underground) came to town. On September 3, 75 of them drove to Pittsburgh for a practice run for "Days of Rage." The weathermen and weatherwomen were affiliated with Students for a Democratic Society (SDS), and took their name from Bob Dylan's lyric, *You don't need a weatherman to know which way the wind* blows.

Twenty-six weatherwomen got arrested after antiwar slogans such as "Ho lives" and "Free Huey"[*] were spray-painted on South Hills High School's main entrance doors. I got a call from one of the leaders being held in the Allegheny County Jail asking for legal help. I was a little uncertain how to respond or whether I should pass the decision on to the ACLU board, so I called Tom Kerr, President of the statewide ACLU.

"Hey, Tom, 26 weatherwomen got arrested at an antiwar protest at South Hills High."

"What were the charges?"

"With 26 of them, I don't know exactly," I said, "but I think the charges were riot, inciting a riot and disorderly conduct."

"Hmmm," Tom said, "our old friend the overbroad and vague disorderly conduct ordinance. Was there any actual disorderly conduct?"

"I don't think so," I said, "just the usual picketing, singing and chanting, unless the spray painting and bare breasts constitute disorderly conduct."

"What's this about spray painting?"

"Well, the front doors of South Hills High are now covered with anti-war slogans."

"Spray painting certainly isn't specifically mentioned in the disorderly conduct ordinance," Tom pointed out, "but the key issue is whether political speech, applied to public property with a spray paint can, loses its character as free speech and becomes property damage. I appreciate their guts in fighting that dreadful war, but we can't let it influence our decision."

"I did a quick check of Supreme Court cases before calling but couldn't find anything quite on point," I said.

"Well," he said, "the court used to follow the test Justice Oliver Wendell Holmes set forth in the *Schenck v. United States* (249 US 47) of 1919, restricting free speech when there was a clear and present danger of evils which the government had a right to prevent. Since the *Douds* case in 1950, (*American Communications Ass'n v. Douds*, 339 US 382), the supremes have allowed a balancing test when speech clashes with other governmental interests. You might think the

---

[*] Ho Chi Minh, the Vietnamese independence leader, and Huey Newton, an incarcerated Black Panther Party leader and author of *Soul on Ice*.

women's case would have a better chance under that test, but the new test has usually been applied to help the government restrict speech. Under either test, I think we would lose this one in court. Not that the ACLU is limited by what a majority of the Supreme Court justices thinks."

"What do you think about running in a high school with bare breasts?" I asked.

"That seems to me to be a distraction from the real issues. Bare breasts are more likely to cause high school students to gawk than to riot. It could be considered symbolic speech. Women's bare breasts are not obscene, you can see them on statues all over town. That's our community standard."

Professor Kerr was a great teacher, his words always more articulate than my thoughts, particularly on the subject of bare breasts. But he was telling me things I already knew.

I said, "I lean a little to the actual words of the Constitution, 'No law restricting freedom of speech.' But here they had many ways to express their views without spray-painting the school doors."

"I'm with you there," Tom said, "I think you should run this decision by the other members of the executive committee. My vote is for taking the case. If the other committee members agree on rejecting the case, please let the young women know why. I expect that the police don't particularly like them and may more clearly violate the Constitution in the next round."

A majority of the ACLU executive committee voted to provide an attorney for the women. Mike Louik took the case. When it was called I heard that the magistrate's court was packed with police. They were crowding for a good view, apparently hoping for another baring of the breasts. For his part, the magistrate refused to permit the 26 to leave Pennsylvania on the pending disorderly conduct charges. The ACLU argued that this was excessive bail and a violation of the federal right to travel. The Pennsylvania Supreme Court reversed the magistrate, upholding the ACLU's position that the young women be permitted to leave on bail.

Later the weatherwomen handed out leaflets outside Taylor Allderdice High School, conduct clearly protected by the Constitution, but for which they were convicted of disorderly conduct. Again the ACLU defended their free speech rights and appealed the convictions.

On Monday, March 2, 1970 at a townhouse house at 18 West 11th Street in Greenwich Village, New York weathermen and women accidentally detonated a nail bomb killing themselves and everyone in the building. With this action, only six months after their practice run in Pittsburgh, the weather group turned and lost credibility with me. They became the weather underground and, in retaliation for military actions in Vietnam, staged a series of bombings of symbolic governmental buildings.

As usual, William Shakespeare pretty well summed it up. On a battlefield in "Henry VI, Part 3," a Son enters bearing the body of his father, whom the Son has killed, only to confront a Father entering opposite bearing the body of a son whom the entering Father has killed. Says the surviving Son, *Ill blows the wind that profits nobody.*

Regarding women's rights, one thing has remained constant. The Equal Rights Amendment has been introduced in the United States Congress continuously since 1923. The proposed Amendment states: "Equality of rights under the law shall not be denied or abridged by the United States or by any state on account of sex." For me, its adoption remains one of our most important unfinished projects.

15. *Bondsmen, Bribes & Jailed Welfare Mothers*

A continuing goal within the ACLU was to reform the magistrate courts and the bail bonding process. The Eighth Amendment to the United States Constitution provides, "Excessive bail shall not be required." When I started at the ACLU, all the Pittsburgh magistrates were non-lawyers and probably had never read that phrase. Generally they seemed to do what the police wanted. They kept signed but otherwise blank arrest and search warrants in a drawer for the convenience of the police, so that the magistrate need not be disturbed when off duty. These were like blank checks written on the Constitution of the United States.

Bail bonds were one of the greatest barriers to equal justice for the poor. The middle-class defendant could afford to pay a bondsman's premium and secure a speedy release from jail. The poor defendant, who could not afford the bond premium, might languish in jail for months awaiting trial. Some indigent defendants were innocent or were not guilty of some of the offenses with which they were charged. Often, they would spend more time in jail for lack of a bail bond than they would have spent had they falsely pled guilty. And it wasn't easy to prepare for a trial from a jail cell.

The amount of bond was set in practical effect by the police in determining the charge. The higher the bond, the greater the bondman's profit. It seemed to be the police who often called the bondsmen. The bondsmen got there faster than the family members or lawyers. The theoretical purpose of a bail bond was to guarantee appearance of the defendant at trial. But once the accused had paid the bondsman's high commission, he would get none of the money back when he appeared at trial. Kickbacks from the bondsmen to the police and magistrates were rumored but hard to prove.

Release on recognizance means that the defendant promises to pay a certain bail amount if he fails to appear at trial. Under this system the defendant provides personal information but does not have to put up any money in advance to get out of jail. This, or a nominal bail amount of perhaps one dollar, would usually be appropriate where there was no real danger that the accused would fail to appear for trial. A person who was released without payment, yet failed to appear at trial, could face an additional criminal charge. With personal information provided by the defendant and verified by court staff, it would usually be easy for the police to pick up the defendant and jail him if he failed to appear at trial.

In the magistrates courts of that time the use of release on recognizance or nominal bail did not appear to exist. It seemed logical that this had something to do with the large amounts of cash that were being generated in the bail bond process.

During the time I worked for the ACLU, Paul Wahrhaftig, a young lawyer, arrived in town to work for the American Friends Service Committee. This was the same Quaker organization that had given me my start in civil rights activism when I was in high school. Paul became the primary advocate for bail reform and we worked closely together. One creative example was a non-profit, charitable bail bonding company backed by property of the Bidwell Presbyterian Church. It was one step in breaking the corrupt cycle.

The corruption that was then going on came to light a few years later. Sam Meyers was convicted on October 28, 1977 by a federal jury of running a bail bond kickback scheme where between 1970 and 1975, $750,000 was paid to magistrates and constables. His co--conspirator, Steve Levitt, pled guilty. Bail bondsman Levitt testified that he made kickback payments to 31 magistrates and four constables. He testified that magistrates altered the amount of bonds to increase the share of kickbacks they would receive.

One of the magistrates caught in the bribery scandal was Albert C. Pantone. In his appeal from his conviction, the Court of Appeals summarized the trial testimony of Levitt:

> "The government's chief witness was Stephen Levitt, who had pleaded guilty to a violation of 18 USC §§ 1962(d). Levitt testified that he operated a bail bond agency in Pittsburgh from February 1970 through May 1975, writing surety bonds for persons charged with crimes in Western Pennsylvania. Early in 1970 he made arrangements with various magistrates to pay a fifty percent kickback of the surety bond premium, if they referred bond business to Levitt's new agency. Levitt usually posted an invalid bond—either a worthless property bond or a surety bond without an appropriate power of attorney—for persons referred to him at the time of arraignment. By means of such an arrangement, Levitt avoided making any premium payment to Stuyvesant Insurance Company, the principal surety. Inherently, this scheme encouraged the magistrate to require a surety bond at an amount as high as but no higher than the accused party could afford. The magis-

trate and Levitt benefited from the dismissal of cases, for the cost of a valid power of attorney, which was required if the case was held for trial, was thereby eliminated. Also, surreptitious reductions of bonds were made without any refund to bond clients, a procedure that enabled Levitt and the magistrates to obtain an extra profit. Levitt testified to the regular payment of kickbacks in the form of cash payments placed in envelopes that were delivered by him to the magistrates. On occasions when Levitt did not personally pay the magistrate, envelopes containing cash were delivered by his employees or picked up by the magistrates." (*United States v. Pantone*, 634 F.2d 716 at p.3 [3rd Cir. 1980])

Exposing the corruption helped to bring about reform. The trial court judges in the Pittsburgh area established a bail reform plan in 1972. Pursuant to that, my friend and law school classmate Bill Ivill was hired to head a new agency of the court. Its purpose was to assist the court in determining whether bail in more than a $1.00 amount was necessary. If bail was necessary to assure the presence of the defendant at trial, ten percent of the bail amount would be paid by the accused, but that would be returned, less a $10.00 service fee, when the accused appeared in court. Bail bond companies also charged a ten percent fee but did not return it.

Similarly we worked to revise city ordinances, like disorderly conduct, which were often applied in conflict with First Amendment rights. When a new disorderly conduct ordinance was proposed I was invited to submit comments, which generally were accepted. Since I had worked during a law school summer "vacation" in the City of Pittsburgh Law Department, I was in a good position to submit meaningful comments. For example, at my suggestion the new ordinance provided that peaceful picketing was not disorderly conduct.

One severe example of the misuse of the bail bond process occurred when the Allegheny County Attorney, Robert W. Duggan, adopted a policy that bond should be set at $10,000 each and every time there was an alleged assault on a police officer. In our constitutional system a person is presumed innocent until proven guilty. A fine is not to be imposed until after a finding of guilt. The purpose of bail is to guarantee that the accused will appear for trial, not to punish the accused or to impose a fine. One Saturday night there was a loud party. Some of those attending were mothers receiving aid-for-dependent-children. The police were called and there was some pushing and shoving. The result was that the welfare mothers were confined to jail on $10,000 bond. They would likely stay in jail for several months pending the scheduling of their trials. These welfare mothers were unlikely to skip town. They had lived in Pittsburgh all their lives. They could lose their welfare payments if they left town and they hardly had enough money to take off. They had children to care for. I handled the appeal of the bond.

One central problem was how to get the case before an appellate court. The normal route was to file an appeal. But the rules for scheduling and briefing appeals meant that it could take years for the case to get to the appellate judges. All the while the women would reside in jail. My mind went back to Mississippi where I had worked on the same problems of procedure. While there, I had researched ancient writs inherited in America from the chancery courts of England. Recalling that, I delved into the dark recesses of the Pitt law library, seeking out ancient remedies again to speed things up. I wrote it all up elegantly, half in Latin. In the end the Pennsylvania Supreme Court said forget the English history. They just expedited the appeal and freed the welfare mothers.

I was actually disappointed in the result. There had never been a decision from the United States Supreme Court on the issue of bail bonds. My goal was to lose in the Pennsylvania Supreme Court but to win in the United States Supreme Court. This was the mark of an unsophisticated and inexperienced lawyer.

16. Individual Rights

I had a perpetual ACLU client. Wherever he went he was arrested. The reasons for the arrests were really his appearance. The arrests did not make much sense from a constitutional point of view. For his time, he was unique in Pittsburgh. He was a Black hippie. His skin was quite dark and he wore brightly colored, elfin clothes. Imagine a version of Jimi Hendrix without the guitar. He didn't fit in with the hippies and he didn't fit in with the Blacks, not to mention the whites or the police. When a police officer looked at him he would automatically see a crime. But he would have difficulty figuring out just what crime. Together we challenged many old ordinances, such as loitering (defined as doing nothing).

The outlying towns were often the best locations for our law reform efforts. In the City of Pittsburgh, the city lawyers would dismiss the charges against our hippie client, depriving us of the chance to make a legal challenge to wipe the ordinance off the books. An ancient city ordinance in McKeesport, a steel town at the confluence of the Monongahela and Youghiogheny Rivers, prohibited "disorderly conduct" but failed to define the term. The arresting officer could not testify to any disorderly action committed by the Black hippie. Common Pleas Judge J. Warren Watson declared the ordinance unconstitutional. It was void for vagueness. The judge pointed out that laws must be specific enough to inform persons of common intelligence what is, and what is not, prohibited.

One of our ACLU Board members was Richard Thornburgh, who later became a Republican Governor of Pennsylvania and Attorney General of the United States. He got me into a little trouble with J. Edgar Hoover.

I wrote to the FBI requesting my file. I was just curious if I had one. They wrote back saying that there was no specific file on me, but if I would list all the organizations that might have files containing my name, they would do another search. I obliged, listing all the organizations to which I had belonged, including the Boy Scouts. When I listed the ACLU, a letter from an FBI informer to J. Edgar Hoover turned up in that file. It objected to Richard Thornburgh being appointed as United States Attorney. The informant had picked up from my letterhead that Thornburgh was on the board of the Greater Pittsburgh ACLU and the letter writer regarded that as too leftist. So it was

Richard Thornburgh who got me the honor of being named in an FBI file.

We counseled many young men regarding their draft rights and obligations and represented conscientious objectors at draft board hearings and prosecutions. One young man was referred to me by Bill Kunstler, who remembered me from Mississippi. I was flattered that Kunstler even knew of my existence. The young man was applying for conscientious objector status, offering to serve in the military, but only in a non-combatant role such as that of a medic (a very dangerous duty). Because the draft board had already refused the claim, it seemed like a hopeless case. The right to counsel was always denied in draft board proceedings and we decided to contest that. I sent a tough volunteer attorney, Paul Hammer, to the hearing. Along with Paul, I sent a minister. The board forcefully barred Paul from the hearing. (I think Paul made a bit of a fuss.) We were all quite surprised when the draft board granted the young man conscientious objector status.

As ACLU director in Pittsburgh, I also worked on several death penalty cases, notably those of three Black teenagers from Pittsburgh who were sentenced to death in Harrisburg, Pennsylvania. My Mississippi experience, where race dominated everything, continued to infuse my world view, and my work on the death penalty would continue in the next phase of my career, as I resigned my Pittsburgh ACLU position in 1970 to become Assistant Dean at the new Arizona State University College of Law at Phoenix. About two years later, in 1972, the United States Supreme Court changed the whole death penalty scheme in the case of *Furman v. Georgia,* 408 US 238.

17. *Looking Back: A Chinese Princess Can't Change Nell*

My girlfriend Nancy and I were a couple during much of my time with the Greater Pittsburgh ACLU.* We wedded shortly before the move to Phoenix, but our marriage ended amicably in another few years. Around the mid-'70s I formed a new serious romantic relationship with Claire, a bright and beautiful Chinese-American girl whom I took to Pittsburgh to meet my parents and my two earliest, closest, neighborhood childhood friends, Jay Carson and Perrynell MacGregor McMahon. Perrynell's name was composed of that of her father, Perry McMahon, and her mother, Nell MacGregor McMahon.

Perrynell's mother Nell was both a wonderful, exceedingly loyal, neighbor to the English-Welsh-American Venables two mansions away and a constant source of friction on issues of race. Nell's very open and volatile prejudices encompassed Blacks, Jews, Catholics and just about any other ethnicity outside her own, though she seemed to dispense individual exceptions to neighbors like Nick Niccolini, the amiable Italian-American warehouseman who, along with his non-Italian wife, Scotty, lived in a small apartment in the mansion between ours and the McMahons'. When I left Mississippi I had promised myself to try to bring about some change in Nell.

Nell's husband Perry shared many of her prejudices but had more self-control. He was a newspaper reporter and editorial writer, a tall, blond, blue-eyed West Virginian who taught me woodworking. By virtue of his job and charming personality, Perry seemed to know everyone in Pittsburgh. I knew he was a hero from the oil portrait of him lounging in uniform in the Philippines in World War II, but he would never talk about the war.† In face-to-face encounters, gentlemanly Perry always (and Nell usually) treated those they considered inferior with courtesy and respect. Thus, by their conduct, I think they enabled Perrynell to grow up without their degree of prejudice.

---

* They had some adventures together tailing private security guards who thought they were entitled to harass Black pedestrians especially in certain parts of the city. —AV

† I was told early on (and military records confirm) that he'd been a lieutenant-grade news reporter there and, in his only chance encounter with a solitary Japanese soldier, both had quickly turned tail. Decades later, Nell remembered him as a captain heroically saving younger men in combat. —AV

Nell didn't mind saying herself that she had been a gorgeous young socialite woman with flaming red hair. Perrynell, a mischievous tomboy, likewise had beautiful, auburn-brown tresses. The only girl my age in the neighborhood, she was effectively my sister. I spent many happy hours at the McMahons', often playing Chinese checkers and later canasta with Perrynell, Jay, and Nell, or just sitting on the lofty back porch of their partially rented-out mansion, listening as Nell prattled on.

Nell was inwardly tormented, and as she aged I think her rages and general imbalance worsened and became more open. Most hurt in our neighborhood by Nell's outspoken disgusts, I thought, were Jay and Mattie Belle Herring, though Nell generally treated Mattie herself with courtesy as the domestic of her Venable neighbors.

Jay was the creative leader of the white "Little Rascals" sort of gang that played in our large backyard and sometimes around Jay's smaller, more elegant home across Kentucky Street from the McMahon's lower property line. The Carsons acquired the first neighborhood television on which we watched the old-time movie clips on "Howdy Doody." The rest of that show was too childish for us, and Jay didn't like us to say how much he looked like Howdy Doody. There was a bowl of salted peanuts waiting by his father's easy chair every day when Mr. Carson got home from work. While Mrs. Carson was a large, assertive Catholic (pretty tolerant unless we tried to touch the peanuts), Mr. Carson was a small Protestant, always quiet (unless, again, his peanuts were raided).

Both Perry and Nell supported me completely. It was, perhaps, both more and less than the relationship of parents to a son. Like jazz singer Mose Allison's magical seventh son of a seventh son, I was "the only one." Not even handsome blond Jay received as much love and encouragement from then as I did, most likely because he was being raised in his mother's religion.

Nell identified herself as a Republican, despite Lincoln's having been the worst President in American history. She was often fraught about Blacks and detailed their faults in front of Mattie. Was she oblivious to Mattie's presence because Mattie was a servant? Nell said she loved Mattie. Perhaps some mental twist had allowed her to decide that Mattie wasn't Black.

When sweeping the sidewalk at the foot of her property, Nell would stop, stare, and shudder as a few Black grade-school kids walked by on the other side of Kentucky Street in the uniforms of

Catholic Sacred Heart. For Nell, this was a double whammy: Catholic, Black children right there across her street.

I felt that Nell told the truth as she perceived it. When I was in grade school I was trying to figure out where babies came from. One day when we were returning home from church I asked my parents, "If a man and a woman were living together, but they were not married, could they have children?"

The response I got was, "Well, I hope *you* will never do that."

"No, no," I said, "I wouldn't do that."

That didn't answer my question, so I asked Mrs. McMahon, "If a man and a woman were living together, but they were not married, could they have children?" She said "Yes." Since that was all I wanted to know, I was completely satisfied with the answer.

A few years later I saw a book about sex that Nell had given Perrynell to read and asked whether I could read it, too. Mrs. McMahon said she would need to ask my mother if that was okay. She did, it was, and so I received my sex education from a scientific book.

As we grew older, Perrynell and I would go to parties and dances together partly because we enjoyed each other's company and partly because we were a team. If there was a boy there she liked, I would see to it that they met. She did the same for me with girls. It wasn't that we weren't sexually attracted to each other. It was just that we never both fell for each other at the same time. Anyway, we avoided a physical relationship and, as a result, stayed "brother and sister" forever.

I knew all along that Nell's prejudices were wrong, and Perrynell could not accept them any more than I could. From my parents I had learned the rightness of accepting all human beings. My Scoutmaster father worked hard to recruit Black leaders into a previously all-white troop. My mother and Nell had words about Nell's racist comments. I wasn't there, but I gathered the substance from things they each said later. After that Nell would preface her racist remarks with, "Now I know your parents disagree, but...."

Nell expressed particular disdain for the "shanty boat Irish." Because Mrs. Carson came from a middle-class, Irish Catholic family (while Mr. Carson came from wealthy English Protestants) Mrs. McMahon frequently told us (out of Jay's hearing) that Jay's Irish mother was beneath us. Many years later Perrynell told me she'd discovered that, many generations back, her father Perry was of Scottish but also regrettably *Irish* descent.

In my family I came upon a similar shame. My great-grandmother Illston had said that her ancestors came from all the countries of western Europe *except* Ireland. Yet Lowell Pangburn, an Irish ancestor of hers and mine had been sent to America with the British army to put down the revolution. But Lowell Pangburn hated the British and deserted them to join up with revolutionary hero Ethan Allen and the Green Mountain Boys. Ethan Allen expressed their philosophy:

> "If we have not fortitude enough to face danger, in a good cause, we are cowards indeed, and must in consequence of it be slaves. Liberty and Property; or slavery and poverty, are now before us, and our Wisdom and Fortitude, or timidity and folly, must terminate the matter."

Pangburn was then captured by the British and imprisoned on an island in the middle of a frozen river. He fashioned skates from kitchen knives, fixed them to his boots and skated away with British bullets flying. He rejoined Ethan Allen and fought at Fort Ticonderoga in the first American capture of a British fort. How could one not be proud to have such an Irish ancestor?

I had trouble understanding why some people like Nell or my own great-grandmother hated the Irish or denied that part of themselves. Irish Americans looked pretty much like Scottish Americans. Both were English-speaking Celtic Christians from the same part of the world,

I think Nell's prejudice came from wanting to be better than other people. She was a beautiful woman whose elegant, bygone oil portraits hung on the walls of her home. She seemed to view herself as being at the top of the world socially, although her reality became that of a middle-class, stay-at-home housewife and mother. She risked real or imagined disgrace from "high society" people as prejudiced as she, should anyone have discovered her husband's Irish roots.

I tried to soften Nell by telling her of my struggles to end racism in Pittsburgh and Mississippi. She would listen politely, but didn't seem to change. My last attempt to convert her from her racist ways came not in the form of an argument but in the form of a person.

That attempt involved Claire. In 1973[*] I had taken a year's leave from teaching in Phoenix to work for the Children's Defense Fund in Cam-

---

[*] After Gil's separation from Nancy.

bridge, While in the Boston area I lived with Claire, whom I regarded as a Chinese princess.

We went on a visit to Pittsburgh. I knew that my parents would love her; to them, race was not an issue. What *did* worry me was whether we, as an unmarried couple, could stay in the same room in their house. That question was answered when my mother offered us the beautiful bedroom with the large bay window that had been reserved for years for a daughter.

Claire didn't call herself a princess, but my regard for her in that respect had more basis than just my affection.

Her father's 19th-century, several-times-great-uncle, Li Hung Chang, had been prime minister or viceroy to the empress dowager of China. Li had started from nothing and worked his way up to the highest educational examination level in China. He then rose to the rank of general, ending several attempted rebellions. When the Tongzhi Emperor died in 1875, Li took his army into the capital and placed the Guangxu emperor on the throne under the tutelage of the two dowager empresses. He had his ups and downs with the empress dowager, Tz'u His, but for more than thirty years (from 1875 until the effective end of the Imperial Court of China in 1911), Li was overall the most influential man in the Chinese royal court, controlling, among other things, China's foreign policy.

The United States' *Chinese Exclusion Act* of 1882 had banned most emigration to America from China, souring the two countries' relations. A Republican-led Congress had passed the bill at the urging of the party's west coast wing and with support from Democrats around the country, who felt that Chinese laborers undercut the wages of white men. In a triumphal tour of America in 1896, Li spoke out against the ban. In his journal he wrote:

> "For years my people have been barred out of this rich country not because they were criminals or had leprosy, but just because they were born in China. If the same persons had been born in Japan or Korea or India or England they would have been let pass through the emigrant gates. And yet, I was born in China, and these Americans, high and low, pay me the honour and attention due a visiting monarch. I will see if this cannot be changed somewhat."

And later:

"The great United States has been our friend in the past, even though she shut out the emigrants, and she will be our strong friend in need some day."

Between 1908 and 1938, Claire's father and five other family members came to the United States, not as laborers or immigrants, but as students at Brown University. On obtaining degrees they returned to positions of responsibility in China, generally with the Bank of China.

Another of Claire's ancestors was a viceroy and governor of four provinces, two at a time. Claire's paternal grandfather was the president of the Bank of China and her maternal grandfather was its vice president. They were much involved in financing the industrialization of China and the building of railroads.

Claire's family lost everything to the communist revolutionary victory in 1949 and fled Peking for Taiwan. When they left again from Taiwan for America, Claire, as a little girl, lost the two "anas" or wet nurses who had lovingly attended her every need.

In America she became the middle-class daughter of a chemistry professor, a college graduate and, when I met her, the secretary of a law professor friend of mine. She was my kind of girl, typically dressed in overalls and flannel shirts. We cross-country skied in Canada, backpacked in the Rockies and floated the length of the Grand Canyon in oar-powered rafts with David Brower.

Before introducing Claire to the McMahons, I visited Nell alone to tell her Claire's background. Since Nell hated communists, I figured I could gain a few points in advance.

Claire made a stunning and gracious appearance, even in Levi's rather than robes. Her face resembled those in ancient scrolls of the Chinese court, except for a little upward kink in her nose. (Her father attributed the kink in *his* nose to the 13th century visit of Marco Polo's expedition to his ancestral town.)

Nell maintained her prejudice, but in a way that surprised me. She said Claire was beautiful, intelligent and charming, and she could see why I cared for her. To that she added, "The Chinese on average are more intelligent than we are. Their centuries-old culture is superior to ours. They will never accept you. It's wrong to mix the races."

I didn't know how to respond and never tried to change Nell again.

Next, Claire and I were off to visit her parents in Tennessee. After Nell's comments, I was a little apprehensive about how they might receive me. Claire reassured me that the issue was behind them. Her oldest sister, Elaine, had married a Chinese scientist, but the next sister, Daphne, had fallen in love with Richard, a white artist. Her parents had objected strongly, but Daphne and Richard married, and in time he had been accepted into the family.

I wanted to be especially polite, so I asked Claire if I could take her parents a little house gift. She suggested that a box of tea would be traditional. I was a little worried at that. I knew enough not to select anything that came in a tea bag, but how could I choose a great tea for a Chinese couple with roots in the royal court? Then the idea came to me of an American tea that both Claire and I liked.

"What about Red Zinger?" I asked Claire. Red Zinger was a fruity, kind of countercultural herbal tea. There wasn't any real tea in it.

"Hmm. Red Zinger. Could be a good idea. If they don't like it, at least they will appreciate the thought."

I gave them the Red Zinger, explaining that I didn't expect it to come up to the standards of Chinese tea, but that Claire and I liked it. They tried it and claimed to like it, too.

Claire's father, Paul Bien, was both a chemistry professor and a classical Chinese scholar, daily practicing his graceful calligraphy and enjoying poetry and literature. How could two chemists not hit it off? For a while, Claire's mother held back. Basically, she had been hiding from the uncivilized and criminal American world ever since she had been forced to flee the safety of the royal court. But I think she was beginning to like me, too.

Paul Bien told me some stories of Great Uncle Li, including this one about the origin of the American dish called chop suey. (I know there are rival explanations.)

As prime minister, everywhere Li went in America he was entertained at lavish banquets. Inevitably they served steak and potatoes. Li grew tired of this fare and asked his host, "Couldn't you once serve Chinese food?"

"I would be happy to," was the reply, "but my chef doesn't know how to prepare it."

Li said, "It's easy. You chop up some vegetables in little pieces and stir-fry them. Then you stir-fry little chopped pieces of chicken or pork and then cook them all together with some soy sauce."

The American chef followed those guidelines. Available vegetables included celery, bean sprouts, onions and mushrooms. Unsure what to do with the strong-tasting soy sauce, he made a sauce of corn starch and water and added a little soy sauce to it. Not knowing that the Chinese eat rice from rice bowls, he dumped the whole dish over a pile of rice.

Americans crowded to see Prime Minister Li everywhere he went and "chop suey" (chop soy) became immensely popular. Chop suey restaurants sprang up across America. Chop suey is still eaten by Americans, but not by the Chinese.

As we left, Claire's father presented me with a small box of Chinese tea, the most wonderful that could be imagined—delicate, aromatic and flavorful. Each leaf was rolled up like a tiny cigar, and opened slowly when the hot water was poured in. Paul said it was very rare and had been smuggled out of China. At that time, our government had banned all trade with communist China. Claire's parents had received the tea as a gift from a very rich man who was still in love with Claire's mother. Not only did it make a very fine present, but Paul was happy to be getting it out of his house.

18. Children's Defense & the "Mean Streets" of New Bedford

Working a year in Boston, I was in transition not only in personal relationships but in the framework of my career. No fault for my restlessness lay with the new ASU College of Law in Phoenix. Relationships there were very collegial among a faculty drawn from around the country, a close social circle that both partied and worked together. The curriculum was rearranged with the core courses in the first two years. This freed third-year students for a wide variety of courses and internships. To them I was able to teach what I wished, most of which could have been titled "How to Use the Law to Change the World." While at ASU and afterward, I continued to be active in civil liberties, serving as President of the Arizona Civil Liberties Union.

But I was headed back to more active practice and also wanted to take the sort of year-off that the Children's Defense Fund embodied.

The CDF had just been founded by Marian Wright Edelman, with whom I had worked in Mississippi. From the start it was an amazing organization, melding talents in a different and more complete way than I had seen before. It was a public interest law firm that added large groups of specialists who functioned in different spheres. There was a group in Washington DC that specialized in the administrative process. They would draw up and get adopted regulations that profoundly advanced the basic goals set by legislation. They would also get action out of federal agencies. Another group, primarily professors at Harvard and MIT, designed massive research studies. What was unique for a public interest law firm was that everything was based on the research, not on some lawyer's random idea. The head of it all, Marian also raised money from foundations that made the whole thing float.

The big foundation-funded project when I arrived was "Children out of School in America." Marian's projects were always well titled. Not, "What's wrong with Education" or "Inequality in the Schoolhouse." The title itself tells you the basics of what is wrong. Children should not be out of school. How could anyone disagree?

For this study the scientists selected census tracts around the United States where census data identified a high proportion of children of mandatory school age who were not in school. Seventy-seven-item questionnaires were created for door-to-door surveys, to find out why high numbers of children were not in school. The census tracts were selected to reflect the "other" America, from urban poor, to southwestern pueblo, to Appalachian poverty.

We staff lawyers at CDF were writing long research memos on subjects related to the project, such as disciplinary exclusions from school and special education. We were also handling various individual cases as they came in. Meanwhile, for the moment, other staff were doing the long, hard, door-to-door work.

Dan Yohalem, one of the staff lawyers, and I represented a girl with cerebral palsy who had been excluded from a Boston-area school. Ironically, she was the only child in her family who really wanted to go. This pre-teen girl made a big impression on me, staggering across the family living room with a big grin on her face in the hope of returning to school. She was being excluded because she couldn't control her urine, and the teacher refused to change diapers. We had a hearing before the school board which decided that the girl belonged in school. The eventual solution was for the district to supply a teacher's aid.

While I was working at CDF, a young lawyer named Hillary Rodham was added to the staff. She was a very pleasant, sophisticated recent graduate of Yale Law School. The Law Students' Civil Rights Research Council had given Hillary a grant in 1970 to work for Marian's Washington Research Project (the predecessor to CDF). So I'd been only five years ahead of her in working for Lizcrick. Still, she seemed young and innocent, as well as brilliant. She had the office next to mine in the old Victorian home that housed the CDF in Cambridge. Marian had worked closely with Hillary at Yale and in the Washington Research Project and saw a special place for her in the organization. Hillary seemed a bit lonesome, working on the weekends, doing nothing for fun. I found out that she had a boyfriend in Arkansas. One crisp New England fall day when I was going to pick apples with a friend and her children, I invited Hillary along but she declined.

The Children out of School door-to-door work was behind schedule, so Marian drafted all the lawyers to work on it. We spread out door-to-door in poverty-stricken census tracts around the country. One neighborhood of immigrants Hillary and I worked in was New Bedford, Massachusetts, which was largely Portuguese-speaking people from the islands of Cape Verde. These residents were at least part Black African in origin, but their island culture was unique.

We went there because the dropout rate was among the highest in the nation; Children out of School had found that in the poorest section of New Bedford three-quarters of the 16- and 17-year-olds of Portuguese descent were not in school. Parts of it still looked like a battle zone, three years after serious rioting. Young gangs hung out on the corners. That's who we met on those "mean streets." My guess is that Hillary's experience there improved her street smarts.

We were supposed to work in pairs for safety, but my partner and I generally split up to get the job done faster. To me, having worked in Mississippi and Black neighborhoods of Pittsburgh, it was like home. I didn't see much danger to ourselves on those streets and in those homes. Americans are universally concerned with children being out of school. Cooperation came from all parts as soon as locals learned what we were doing. A particular youth may drop out but still support his brother or sister's choice and right to attend.

In a local restaurant we joined community allies for a lunch of cachupa, the Cape Verdean national dish, a meat stew with hominy, beans, and vegetables. We picked up a little on the culture. The ten remote Cape Verde islands were then still a Portuguese colony seeking independence. Their homeland was poor but very beautiful. On the islands they likely had been farmers with a cooperative and sharing mind set. They were mostly Catholics. Such knowledge made our job easier and safer, as well as more fun.

One day Hillary and I were with Marian in her office, on the first floor of the Victorian, whose large windows looked out on a pleasant residential street. On the wall hung a child's drawing of a tiny boat at sea, along with the words "Dear Lord, be good to me. The sea is so wide, and my boat is so small."

Hillary was hesitating over leaving Cambridge and CDF to join her boyfriend Bill in Arkansas. She loved Bill, but Arkansas was so far from her own world of exciting ideas. Marian said she should go and promised to arrange for Hillary to be able to continue in a meaningful role with CDF, keeping up those contacts in New York City. Then Marian predicted that, of all the young men who wanted to be President, Bill Clinton had the best chance.

It's the second time I was present when Marian predicted the future, this time two decades forward. The first had been in Jackson when she had that lawsuit ready to file, anticipating the mass arrests. For my part, I thought it was ridiculous to think that some hayseed law teacher from Arkansas, who never had held any public office, was going to become President of the United States.

West

19. Executions in the West

As I've mentioned, with the ACLU I had worked on some Pennsylvania death penalty cases. In 1972, when I was assistant dean at Arizona State, the US Supreme Court changed the whole death penalty discussion with the case of *Furman v. Georgia*. (408 US 238).

There was no clear majority, but concurring opinions by the justices focused on the arbitrariness with which death had been imposed, indicating a racial bias against Black defendants. The *Furman* decision forced states to rethink their statutes for capital punishment to assure that the death penalty would not be administered in a discriminatory manner. One of the majority, Justice Potter Stewart, wrote:

> "These death sentences are cruel and unusual in the same way that being struck by lightning is cruel and unusual. For, of all the people convicted of rapes and murders in 1967 and 1968, many just as reprehensible as these, the petitioners are among a capriciously selected random handful upon whom the sentence of death has in fact been imposed. My concurring Brothers have demonstrated that, if any basis can be discerned for the selection of these few to be sentenced to death, it is the constitutionally impermissible basis of race."

It made me think this an opportune time to try to pass a "humane" death penalty law in Arizona. I was opposed to the death penalty in general and particularly to allowing it for ordinary murders, which usually occur between husband and wife or lovers. Often these murders do not involve particularly violent people. Usually the convicted person makes an ideal prisoner. These people stand in contrast with other particularly bad or unpopular types of murderers, including those for hire, repeat murderers, bombers, and killers of cops. My thought was to list the particular types of murder that deserved consideration for the death penalty. This would exclude the types that were better punished by prison terms and would tend to limit the racial prejudice in the administration of the death penalty. It was a halfway step, but one that would go a long way in reducing the use of capital punishment in Arizona.

I put together a team of three: myself, the University of Arizona's assistant dean of the College of Law (whose name I don't remember) and Jack LaSota, then head of ASU's Criminal Law Clinic and later be a Republican Arizona Attorney General. Together we went to the Arizona State Capitol, a big building with a copper dome in downtown Phoenix, where we received a warm reception from the state senate's Republican majority leader, Sandra Day O'Connor. She liked the concept we presented. However, one of the crusty old Republican leaders commented that "letting us participate was like letting the fox into the chicken house." In admonishment, Senator O'Connor responded, "We don't want to see a blood bath in Arizona."

Then as now, everything in the Arizona legislature was controlled by the Republican caucus, and our idea didn't get far. But O'Connor's comment did play a small role in her eventual confirmation as Justice of the United States Supreme Court. As usual, Democrats in Washington were considering opposing a Republican nominee for the court. They figured correctly that I would know Judge O'Connor, and so I received several calls. I related the death penalty story, among other things, and told them not to oppose this conservative with a heart.

20. *Rooted in the Desert*

In 1976, I stopped teaching at ASU and began a private practice to handle as much civil liberties and environmental work as we could afford.* In the fall of 1977, I met Christine Locke in Fish Creek Canyon in the Superstition Mountains. We had both been attracted to a trip led by an ASU geology professor about the volcanic history of the mountains. It was the only Sierra Club sponsored hike that either of us had ever gone on. She was walking down a mountain road with the dust motes dancing around her feet like a cloud of gold. She was dressed in hiking clothes and wore no makeup. Her light brown hair was streaked blond by the sun and hung down straight to her shoulders, a complement to her green eyes.

It must have been love at first sight for me, because Chris said little on the hike. I got her name from the name tags we were luckily, but strangely, required to wear out in the wilds of Arizona. I figured out that she was a California girl and that pretty much clinched it for me. At the end of the day, I didn't want to lose her and apparently she felt the same, so we ended up at my place and have been together ever since.

The only wrinkle was that we seemed almost too much alike. In our minds were the same rainbow colors. We liked the same music: John Prine, Motown, Neil Young, Kate Wolf, and Gram Parsons. We were both white from old Anglo-American families, liberals with graduate degrees, similar religious views, both committed to social change.

We married and bought a house with a red tile roof in a working-class part of the Encanto neighborhood in downtown Phoenix.† Some fifty years before we moved in, the neighborhood had been legally segregated by privately established restrictive covenants on the lots. But, thanks to the legal work of Thurgood Marshall, in 1948 this practice had been declared unconstitutional by the Supreme Court in *Shelley*

---

* Venable, Rice, Lee and Capra. Calvin Lee says this concept of a small firm doing general practice to support such pro bono work was unique in Phoenix at the time.

† Gil came to love the Sonora Desert and he and Chris hiked in it often. Having experienced allergies as a child in Pennsylvania, he also loved the Phoenix air quality as it was some decades ago.

v. Kraemer (344 US 1). The big issue in *Shelley* had been whether racially restrictive covenants were public or private. New residents in Encanto after that case were a mix of Caucasian, Hispanic, African, Asian, and Native American. It was a tolerant neighborhood where some gay and lesbian couples had recently found a comfortable place to live.

We selected our home partly because it was in the attendance area of the excellent, well-integrated, public May Bartlett Heard School. Arizona's schools had once been legally segregated for Blacks and informally segregated by districts that established separate "Mexican Schools." In 1950, United States District Court of Arizona Judge Dave Ling declared the "Mexican School" segregation unconstitutional in *Gonzales v. Sheely,* but segregation of Blacks continued until a local court decision by Judge Fred Struckmeyer in 1953, *Phillips v. Phoenix Union High School.* This was a year before the Supreme Court's historic decision in *Brown v. Board of Education* (1954). Thus, we had benefited from the legal work of others who went before us.

In time, we had two daughters, Elizabeth and Jessica. While Elizabeth was at Heard, she learned that my law partner, Bruce Randall, also had gone to school there, so she asked him, "Did they have electricity there in your day?"

"Sweetie, I'm not *that* old," he said.

Chris led a Girl Scout troop that mirrored the rainbow colors of the neighborhood. I got to go along on camping trips.

Another interest Chris and I shared was special education. As a school psychologist, she was devoted to providing appropriate educational services to handicapped children. At that time many educators seemed to feel that non-handicapped, bright and athletic students were more deserving of precious resources. When she and I had met, I was working on *Eaton v. Arizona,* a class-action lawsuit seeking to establish that the Arizona Constitution granted the handicapped a right to education.

Richard Eaton was a five-year-old Down syndrome child who had been sent home from school in the small Mohave School District No. 16, located in a remote area along the Colorado River. He was a pleasant boy with a round face, almond-shaped eyes, a small nose, and straight fine hair. I met him in the kitchen of his devoted mother Janice, who lacked the education needed to educate Richard herself at home. Richard's father, Dale, worked in the power plant across the river in California. Dale and Janice were fighters, eager to stand up for the educational rights of their son and others like him.

Gil, Chris Locke, Elizabeth, & Jessica, around 1990.

The Children's Defense Fund had given me some experience with right-to-education law. I knew that the Pennsylvania Association for Retarded Citizens had won a lawsuit establishing a right to education for handicapped children in a federal court in Pennsylvania. The decision was based on the equal protection and due process clauses of the US Constitution and thus should be a strong precedent supporting our case. But, as it was not an Arizona case, it would not be binding on Arizona courts.

I started by researching Arizona's state constitution and found the provision that "a free school shall be established and maintained in every school district for at least 6 months a year, which school shall be open to all pupils between the ages of six and twenty-one years." This seemed a nice supplement to federal constitutional provisions that had been used in similar litigation before.

No one else seemed prepared to lead the challenge, and it needed to be done. I enlisted Larry Katz as trial counsel and assembled a team that eventually included Rob Beckett,* Calvin Lee,† Mike Kelly, and Bill Mahoney.

---

* Licensed in Arizona in 1975, Rob's first employment there was as legal services di-

On December 6, 1974, we filed the *Eaton* case suit in the Mohave County Superior Court seeking both a declaration of the rights of Arizona handicapped children to an education and an injunction requiring the district to provide an education for Richard. Since the courthouse wasn't far from "Sin City" Las Vegas, Larry Katz insisted on spending the evening before the trial there. Larry had many favorite spots in Vegas that opened my eyes a bit, so we got no sleep at all. But adrenalin kept us going through the morning trial.

The school district was, in effect, branding Richard an outcast, one "not acceptable" to succeed in normal human dealings. In the past, before they were allowed in school, many mentally disabled children lived at home throughout their lives. As their parents aged and could no longer care for them, they were either taken in by other relatives or placed in institutions. It was unlikely that Richard would achieve academic skills higher than the third grade, but elementary school would teach him social skills that he would need to enter high school and eventually the world of work. Whether employed in a sheltered workshop, flipping burgers or bagging groceries, he would have that all-important skill of congeniality.

Dale and Janice Eaton were straightforward and hard-working and presented well in court. Richard was a pleasant little boy who behaved appropriately. The superintendent lost the case when he testified that the elementary district was spending thousands of dollars on new band uniforms, but couldn't afford to educate one handicapped child. The judge, Frank X. Gordon, issued a ten-day temporary restraining order requiring that Richard be permitted to attend kindergarten with a paid or volunteer aid.

We, the school district and the Arizona State Department of Education all agreed that the department should send a team of experts to assess the situation and evaluate Richard's disabilities and strengths. That team came up with two recommendations. Their preference was that Richard attend the local kindergarten with an aid provided to address his special needs. Their second choice was for the district to provide a two-hour ride across the mountains to Kingman, where a

---

rector of an organization for persons with developmental disabilities. Father of a now grown-up Down syndrome son, his long private practice has focused on the needs of families with members who are substantially impaired.

† Lawyer, artist, Gil's one-time law student at ASU and long-time friend.

teacher educated in special education ran a class for the mentally handicapped. Dale and Janice chose the Kingman class.

With the basic individual problem solved, we needed to decide whether to proceed with the class action allegations or just declare victory and go home. Other handicapped children who were not receiving services appeared, and the Eatons wanted to press forward on a court declaration of constitutional right for others. On the other hand, the mandate in the federal *Education for All Handicapped Children Act of 1974* (P.L.94-142), would soon be going into effect and might obviate another lawsuit.

The *Eaton* case assembled a coalition of supporting organizations: the Association for Retarded Citizens, the Association of Children and Adults with Learning Disabilities, and the Council for Exceptional Children, a professional group.

A team of many professionals and parent leaders met evenings at our home. A standout among them was Dorothy Crawford, mother of two learning-disabled children who had been misdiagnosed and mislabeled in various ways. At that time, learning disability education was a new field. To begin to figure it out, Dorothy had earned a master's degree in special education and, before moving to Arizona, had worked her way up to chairing the California Governor's Advisory Committee on Special Education. She set up a non-profit organization to do federally funded research on learning disabilities and also to develop remedial programs. She and the others who guided our group were wise and experienced. I was their servant.

We decided to press forward on what would become years of hard work. Our chances seemed uncertain for getting both plaintiffs and defendants certified as classes (which is rare), but we succeeded there, gaining class action certifications for the plaintiff class of all handicapped children in Arizona and for the defendant class of all Arizona school districts. This meant that instead of establishing a right for one child in one school district, we could potentially establish rights for all handicapped children in every district and get a court order that would benefit children not named in the lawsuit and also bind districts that hadn't been named.

The representative defendant districts sealed our victory on the class actions by taking what is called a "special action" to the Arizona Supreme Court. In Arizona a special action is a speed-up device that asks the state supreme court to review a trial court decision without waiting for an appeal at the end of the case. In the first step of a special action, the court decides whether it wants to listen to the case. It rarely does, and per usual it refused the districts' request. This was good for us because it led the several trial judges to regard the class action certifications as cemented in the case.

Judge Frank Gordon's elevation to the state supreme court had removed him from the matter, but our new judges (Greer and later Goodfarb) denied all of the districts' many fanciful motions. All three judges seemed to sympathize with the strange idea that handicapped children could benefit from an education. They also had no trouble reading this clear language from the state constitution: "School shall be open to all pupils between the ages of six and twenty-one years." The state attorney general had no trouble reading it and issued a formal opinion, binding on the state agencies and school districts, that handicapped children had a state constitutional right to attend.

The favorable decisions on procedure and substance brought us to the point of settlement. Although we were unable to achieve a global settlement binding on non-participating districts and had to settle with the individual districts that had been named in the suit, on the good side the settlements included provisions not found in previous special education litigation.

The best example of this can be seen in our settlement with the Tucson Unified School District No. 1 of Pima County, the largest district in the state. Tucson USD's special education programs already had an excellent reputation. That quality and compliance with state and federal law was reflected in the first paragraphs of the settlement, which complemented Tucson's existing programs. Further new and important provisions centered on pupil/teacher ratios.

A child is or should be placed in a special education program only when incapable of learning in the regular classroom. Among students with educational disabilities, each child is unique and has special needs in terms of learning. Because some need more individual attention to encourage learning or manage health-related problems, smaller class size is important. Yet no standards existed regarding the size.

As part of the settlement agreement and court order, the Tucson district provided pupil/teacher ratios they deemed adequate to the education of various categories of handicapped students. For example, for Educable Mentally Handicapped pupils the ratio was fifteen per teacher, while the ratio for Visually Handicapped pupils was eight per teacher. The consent order further provided that, "The District may increase the membership in these classes by two pupils after employing a full-time trained paraprofessional to work in the classroom or program."

Since then, no other state in the country has created standards like those the *Eaton* case established. In Tucson, the pupil/teacher ratio standards have stood for many years.

We also focused on the monitoring of special education programs to get some idea what was actually happening in districts around the state. This is done by trained professionals from the State Department of Education, who periodically check to make sure that district programs and records meet legal standards for children with disabilities. Unfortunately, we were not able to make the system monitor pupil/teacher ratios in all districts as we'd brought about in Tucson.

When we began the lawsuit, special education programs in the Department of Corrections were not monitored. Corrections considered itself a separate state agency, not subject to monitoring by the Department of Education. This particularly bothered the Association for Children and Adults with Learning Disabilities because learning-disabled children were ending up in juvenile correctional facilities in disproportionate numbers and then were not receiving appropriate educational services. Afterward, however, in light of federal legal requirements, the special education programs of Corrections were made subject to monitoring by Education.

An important overall impact of the *Eaton* case was to help solidify the mythology that all people are fundamentally equal, a myth that if it is believed, becomes true.

21. Border Lives

When I was a child I would look at my grandfather's globe, with lines and different colors partitioning Earth into separate countries. I knew which one was mine. I knew also that, as an American I was like a Roman in the glory days of Empire, so most of the rest of those colors and borders were mine to cross with ease. As a youth my family took me to Canada and I went to Europe twice. My American dollars dominated and were accepted anywhere. I could go abroad much more readily than foreigners could come here. Well, some could visit, very few stayed. Years later, viewing the earth in photos from space, the lines and colors were gone. That new medium helped me and others imagine a gain in worldwide human equality. The image of a unified earth seems to suggest the fairness of people outside the US traveling equally easily here and staying on when lives are at stake.

In 1982, in the case of *Plyler v. Doe* (457 US 202), the US Supreme Court stepped in that direction by deciding that an illegal alien child is a "person." The Fourteenth Amendment states, "nor shall any State deprive any *person* of life, liberty, or property, without due process of law; nor deny to any *person* within its jurisdiction the equal protection of the laws." In *Plyler* the court held that "intermediate scrutiny" must be applied to determine whether a Texas act denying educational funding for illegal alien children was constitutional. Applying this standard, a majority of the justices held that the Texas act was a violation of equal protection.

In that same year, with death squads active in Central America, I volunteered to represent some refugees (usually several members of an extended family) in asylum proceedings. Like Blacks in the Deep South, brown illegal aliens weren't getting much respect in Arizona.

The first were members of a musical family from El Salvador. For convenience I'll tell the story primarily from the point of view of "Alfonso" (not his real name), a timid, high-school-age musician, short, with dark hair and medium-dark skin. He played a booming six-string, acoustic bass guitarron, a traditional mariachi instrument somewhat like a huge, round-bodied guitar.

To me, Alfonso's appearance suggested substantial indigenous native, Indian blood, which could give him a better chance at asylum because the US State Department recognized that Central American indigenous peoples were being slaughtered for their lands. But Alfonso claimed a Spanish heritage and denied any Indian blood.

In these immigrant asylum cases, we needed to prove that applicants had a well-founded fear of persecution should they return to their country; and we could see a well-founded fear of death. In the two years before Alfonso applied for asylum, five relatives had been murdered.

One had been Alfonso's uncle, a shopkeeper and member of ORDEN, a paramilitary organization formed by the government. Once a person joined ORDEN he was not allowed to quit. Shortly after the uncle decided to do so, people came to his store and shot him.

A second was a cousin, shot and killed when he opened his door to persons who had identified themselves as government authorities. Several months later the third, the cousin's widow, was shot and killed at home.

A fourth, in November 1983, was another uncle, taken from his home by six armed men. The next day his body was found, beheaded.

The fifth was Alfonso's father who, in June 1980, while attempting to come to the US, was picked up by Mexican immigration authorities and deported back to El Salvador. About two weeks later he disappeared. Several weeks later his body was found along a road about thirty miles from the family's hometown, San Miguel. Alfonso, twelve years old at the time, had observed the scene. Three bodies lay in a row. In front of them, posted on a stick, a notice signed "The Death Squad" said, "We have killed one and there are more to be killed." Alfonso saw that his father had been shot in the head and in the left side of the chest. His left arm had been pulled back violently and partially torn off, and the body showed other signs of torture.

These members of Alfonso's family had been personal friends and active congregants of Father Oscar Anulfo Romero, a parish priest in San Miguel (and related to the family by marriage) before he'd been elevated to Archbishop of El Salvador. In March 1980, while saying mass, Romero was assassinated by a death squad.

Alfonso was a professional musician whose grandfather had played the guitar in Father Romero's church. Alfonso's father had also been a professional mariachi player. The uncle who adopted Alfonso after the father's death is also a mariachi player and composer. One of his songs, "The Tragedy of the Desert," tells the story of Salvadoran refugees who died on the arduous trek to America. In El Salvador, this song would have been regarded as seditious.

We presented expert testimony, in the form of an affidavit from former US Ambassador to El Salvador Robert White, that the surviving family's association with an activist portion of the Catholic Church, their association with family members who had already been killed, their prominence as musicians, and in the case of Alfonso, being a young male, would probably single them out for death or persecution if they were deported back to El Salvador. Assembling proof of facts from a war-torn country is not easy, but we were able to submit other affidavits that told the story from the perspective of each of the family members. Varied multiple individual stories can be powerful in combination.

After a hearing, the immigration judge denied the asylum claims of Alfonso and his relatives. I couldn't believe it. I got a temporary stay of the deportations pending an appeal to the Board of Immigration Appeals in Washington. But I could sense the chance of failure at that level, too. Feeling I would be personally responsible if I permitted him and his family to be deported to their deaths, I talked to the experts at the Central American Refugee Project. They told me that one possible reason for the denial was that the immigration judge was just another part of our State Department, and our government was supporting the death squads.

Alfonso was safe for a year or so while his appeal was pending. Finally, the Board of Immigration Appeals ruled in favor of all of the members of his family. From there, Alfonso continued his career as a mariachi musician, safe and with a route ahead to become an American citizen.

On both sides of my family I see a long tradition of not only smuggling other persecuted people across borders but also *being* refugees themselves. My Victorian great-great grandfather Thomas Vater had smuggled himself and his family out of England just in time to escape arrest for radical, pre-Chartist activities. Much further back, one ancestor on my mother's side is *Mayflower* passenger William Brewster. At age 13 in 1580, Brewster was exposed to a free-thinking religious crowd at Cambridge University before becoming a member of the royal court of Queen Elizabeth and serving in the Netherlands aiding Dutch opposition to a Spanish invasion.

Later, William Brewster became an English postmaster and also what was then known as a Separatist (member of a Protestant congregation separate from the Church of England). The people of England had recently been allowed to read the Bible. On doing so, the Separatists had concluded that they were living deep in sin. Furthermore, their neighbors were also living in sin and needed to be told so. This did not make the Separatists popular. The British government jailed them and made their life hard enough in other ways that they decided to escape to the Netherlands, just across the English Channel, where there was freedom of religion.

But they couldn't leave England openly without Royal permission, which was not forthcoming. At that point Brewster turned coyote. Among the ruling Separatist elders, he alone had the diplomatic experience to get them out. The first time they tried to embark, they were arrested and jailed for a month. On a second try a few months later, he got them past the border patrol and safely across.

In the Netherlands William was an illegal alien, "hidden" but teaching Latin at the University of Leiden. He also published religious books which were regarded as treasonous in England. By royal rights, the English King James ordered the Dutch to surrender William's head; but, try as they might, the Dutch insisted they were having trouble finding it.

In time the Separatists became concerned that their children were becoming assimilated into Dutch life and also that war was brewing again with Spain. Again, William Brewster became the coyote and their pastor for a longer journey. Known as Pilgrims, in 1620 they hired a ship and set sail across the Atlantic to what they would call the Plymouth Colony. Before arriving they signed what was called the Mayflower Compact. This pact said that while they would honor their king, they would enact their own "just and equal laws." I feel lucky he made it, in more ways than one.

Well, back to the twentieth century and our Encanto neighborhood of Phoenix: our girls got giardia, and we got instructions not to send them back to school until they were better. Chris and I both had heavy work schedules with fixed appointments. The Central American Refugee Project had been bugging me to take another *pro bono* case. I told them that if they could find someone to babysit sick kids, I would take their case. My rationale was that many people don't like to accept charity and participate better in a team effort when they're giving something in return. The deal turned out fair enough for me: To me, three days of babysitting my sick kids was worth three years of legal work.

So brother and sister Juan and Viviana (not their real names) became my clients and members of our family for a while. They were teenagers who had been sent by their parents from Guatemala to America. A doctor and his wife had found them in church, taken them in and dressed them in fashionable American clothes so they wouldn't be noticed. But somehow immigration officials noticed, and they were being deported back to Guatemala. When I filed their asylum claim, the deportation proceeding was stopped, pending resolution of the claim. In the meantime we taught them how to eat American food and play badminton in Encanto Park.

As with Alfonso's family, in order to stop deportation we had to show a well-founded fear of persecution in their homeland. I saw a basic case for asylum in the facts that their sister had been raped by a Guatemalan Army squad and the boy next door had been forced into the Army as a child. But I couldn't get any documentation of those events. The main reason for danger to them in Guatemala, and the reason they were sent north, was their father's work. He was a truck driver who worked for the Catholic Bishop of Guatemala. His job was to carry staple foods, supplies and produce back and forth to the communal farms run by the Catholic church. In addition to the danger of driving the countryside during an ongoing war, the Guatemalan government, and its death squads distrusted the communes and the Catholic Church.

Juan and Viviana's case was much weaker than Alfonso's. They didn't have the group of family members to bolster the claim through multiple affidavits. Their parents and other close family members had not been assassinated. The violent acts were merely rape and the forcing of a neighbor child into the army. I had to expect to lose again at the initial hearing, as I had with Alfonso. This expectation was hard to bear because I had become very fond of the children. After a sure loss at the hearing I didn't know what to expect on appeal, but I remained optimistic. By then I'd probably memorized Michael Stipe's (R.E.M.) lyric, *Not everyone can carry the weight of the world*, but at that point after Mississippi, I still felt I could do it.

Getting supporting documentation from war-torn Guatemala for any of the case was hard, so I went to my friend Bill Mahoney, who agreed to be co-counsel for free. I didn't even have to mow his grass or clean his pool. I would do all the paperwork, and he would help with strategy and politics.

Bill also happened to be a former ambassador to Ghana in the Kennedy Administration and the attorney for Thomas J. O'Brien, the Catholic bishop of Arizona. He suggested we take the kids to see the bishop. I started to hope O'Brien would write a letter about the jeopardy of the Catholic Church in Central America or about Juan's desire to be a priest. After meeting with Juan and Viviana, Bishop O'Brien wrote a very simple letter that asked our government to be considerate to these children. It didn't mention danger, it didn't mention Guatemala, but by silent implication it established a link between two bishops who were concerned for these children.

Again we lost before the hearing officer and tasted the prospect of death. Again I appealed and we ended up winning before the Board of Immigration Appeals. In the letter explaining its decision to overturn the lower ruling, the board specifically mentioned the bishop's letter. Finally, after the reversal, I could breathe freely again.

We stay in touch with Alfonso, Juan and Viviana. All three are employed and working hard. Juan and Viviana are now each married with children, legal and happy to be living in the land of the free.

The words on the Statue of Liberty, a primary symbol of our nation, are not law, but they are words of the American spirit that should enlighten our immigration laws. "Give me your tired, your poor, your huddled masses yearning to breathe free, the wretched refuse of your teeming shore. Send these, the homeless, tempest-tossed to me. I lift my lamp beside the golden door." I think William Brewster would have liked them.

22. *Prayer on the Mountain*

Stories past and present show that Native Americans have not fared well in terms of equality in America.

Brewster came to know Native Americans as neighbors. In the late 19th century so did my cousin, Ernest Venable Sutton. As Ernie wrote in *A Life Worth Living*, his life began after the Civil War, at the edge of civilization with his parents in the western Ohio home of his grandfather (my great-great) William Venable, about 150 years ago.

Many prominent people visited William Venable at home. Two were Horace Greeley, owner of the *New York Tribune* and Henry Wadsworth Longfellow, then the most popular author in America, who had written many poems against slavery. They came together for dinner and stayed overnight. Ernie didn't care much for Longfellow because his mother made him listen to "Hiawatha" at the expense of the regular fairy stories. He did like Horace Greeley, who had given him a bag of candy hearts with mottos printed on them in red (whereas Longfellow had given him nothing). Besides the gift of candy, Ernie liked Greeley because he was such a funny-looking man.

Another guest was Samuel Clemens. Ernie's mother tried to keep Ernie from listening to him and was glad when the cigar-smoking, whiskey-drinking, gambling, swearing "Mark Twain" left.

But Ernie's parents decided to head west from that comfortable home. After a stay at the National Temperance Colony, where they were defeated by a plague of locusts, they headed across the Dakota plains in two covered wagons. One day in 1878 they camped by a lake. Ernie went off to visit a band of Indians camped nearby. There an old Indian medicine man was attending to a boy with a wounded foot. When Ernie returned to his family camp, his mother was in tears because his baby sister Elsie was sick and, in his mother's view, likely to die.

Ernie was sent to find the old man. It took some time for Ernie to explain by signs what he wanted, having not yet learned to speak the language of the Sioux. The medicine man, nearly naked but painted in red, white and Black, could not have been more concerned and courteous. He went to see the baby, examined her, then built a baby-sized sweat house and made a steam with medicinal plants. On the second day he returned and again performed the treatment. Elsie appeared much better but the old Indian did not stop. Toward evening of the second day he appeared to lose interest and handed the baby back to her mother with a finality that was distressing. He removed the tiny sweat lodge and rode away. Elsie died that night. They buried her by the lake under an oak tree.

Ernie's mother would go no further. They dug a crude house into the bank beside the lake. They later learned that it was Spirit Lake which was a site of peace for the Sioux. There were no towns, no churches, no other white families for many miles, so Ernie grew up in peace with the Sioux, learning their language, customs, religion, and way of life. His Sioux friends tricked him into eating pemmican made from the locusts that to his family were a plague, but to the Sioux a feast.

Two years earlier in 1876, the Sioux had defeated Custer at the Little Big Horn. Many of them, including Sitting Bull, fled to Canada. Eventually, when they were starving, they returned to the reservation in the United States based on a promise from the US government that they would be given the Black Hills. After they returned, the promise was broken.

Sitting Bull traveled with Buffalo Bill Cody's show for four months, then returned to his people. Their plight had worsened due to starvation and disease, particularly measles to which they had no immunity. This was the time of the ghost dancing. Wovoka, a Paiute, preached that the world was old and worn out and must be made new again by a return to the traditional ways. His was a message of peace, and he was seen as a redeemer by the Sioux, but as a false, unchristian messiah by the Indian Bureau. Ernie Sutton saw the militias drilling for a coming Indian war and was concerned that a reign of terror was rapidly developing. By then he had become a printer and had some ability to disseminate the truth.

Ernie decided to travel to the remote area where the spirit dances were held, to bring back an accurate account and offer what help he could in maintaining the peace. It was a difficult trip. He and a companion were stopped by the army at a Missouri River ferry at the reservation border. They hired an Indian guide who, in spite of several difficulties, managed to smuggle them across.

Eventually they made it to a camp at Hump Butte near where the ghost dancing was going on. To Ernie it looked like an old-fashioned camp meeting: folks milling around with hands upraised as if in supplication. Every once in a while, some chap would separate himself and dance alone until he collapsed. Afterward some of the dancers appeared a little wild-eyed, but certainly not warlike. After two days the everlasting jumping up and down became monotonous, and Ernie and his friend headed home. On the way, Ernie thought they should drop in on Sitting Bull.

Sitting Bull was a natural born leader and the original isolationist. He still hated white men. The Indian agents were afraid that Sitting Bull would join the ghost dancers. There was a general feeling among the whites that he should be killed. Ernie went to the crude log cabin where the chief was living. Ernie knocked. The door was opened by a young boy, probably Sitting Bull's son Crow Foot, who would be killed along with Sitting Bull two months later. Sitting Bull could be seen inside. The boy said "No, no white man see him."

Sitting Bull was shot in December 1890. Two weeks later came the massacre of men, women and children at Wounded Knee. Ernie said it might never be known what really happened, the army being in control of the news. That is probably still true today.

Wendsler Nosie is now the tribal chairman of Arizona's San Carlos Apache Tribe. In the fall of 1997 when I represented him, he was heading up a job placement program for unemployed youth on the reservation. He had previously served on the tribal council. Wendsler's daughter was approaching the age for the sunrise ceremony, a four-day ritual that Apache girls experience soon after their first menstruation. The girls take on the physical and spiritual power of White Painted Woman and enter into their role as women of the Apache nation. The ceremony includes songs, prayers, dances, and running toward the four directions. They also give and receive gifts and blessings.

To prepare himself for the ceremony Wendsler decided to climb Mount Graham to pray. This series of majestic blue peaks rises abruptly from the Arizona plains near Safford. To the San Carlos Apache it is sacred and known as Dzil Nchaa Si An. Alpine spruce fir forest is found at its heights. It's highest point is nearly 11,000 feet, so close to the heavens that it has been taken by the University of Arizona as an ideal site for a telescope. This has been resisted by the environmental community because the top of the mountain is the habitat of the endangered Mount Graham Red Squirrel. Many people had been arrested for trespass for going too near the telescope or stepping on the University of Arizona's road. So far, all had been convicted.

Wendsler saw the desecration of the top of Dzil Nchaa Si An as a violation of the sacred, adding to the darkness which was enveloping the world. I saw the same thing, but in different words and images. When Wendsler went to Dzil Nchaa Si An to pray, he avoided the peak where the telescope is located because the machine disrupted the peace of that setting.

The summit is a scene of gnarled trees and open spaces. There are springs and many varieties of plants, some of medicinal value to the San Carlos Apache. Thunderstorms roll in every day. Wendsler said his prayer to God in his native tongue in the traditional manner of his people, out loud. As Wendsler was praying, a thunderstorm came along, with lightning crashing around him. He finished his prayer and, with bolts of lightning striking near him, decided it was time to leave. In his haste to get down, he stepped on the University of Arizona road and was arrested.

In Eastern Arizona, whites despise Apaches more than Blacks. After all, paleface and Apache were still killing each other just a century ago. When Wendsler was growing up, no restaurant or taco stand along the 120 miles between San Carlos and the Indian Health Service Hospital in Phoenix would serve an Apache. Wendsler's trial was to be in Safford, Arizona, a rural town to say the most. Bob Witzeman of the Audubon Society asked me if I would coordinate a defense. I enlisted Jeff Bouma and Bill Foreman, an experienced criminal defense lawyer. On constitutional issues, ASU law Professor Paul Bender assisted us as well. Four talented lawyers is a bit excessive for handling a case in tiny Safford's Justice Court, but it came off fine.

Bill had done a "void for vagueness" brief on a related issue in another case. It needed a lot of work to make it fit our case, but I put it in shape, emphasizing Wendsler's constitutional right to freedom of religion and the *American Indian Religious Freedom Act (42 USC § 1996)*.

The US Supreme Court had not made our situation easy. In the 1988 case of *Lyng v. Northwest Indian Cemetery Protective Association* (485 US 439), it had ruled that the Forest Service could put in a road and harvest timber from a site sacred to Native Americans. The *American Indian Religious Freedom Act* itself was more a policy statement than a legal defense, but it never hurts to have a little policy on your side. In the act, Congress recognized that many traditional Native American religions hold certain lands to be sacred and that such sacred sites are an integral and vital part of Native American religions.

One little blessing was that the University of Arizona had videotaped the entire road, with no one on it, as evidence. This let us make the point that Wendsler had not gone anywhere near the telescope. The judge in fact ruled that the portion of the videotape where the road was near the telescope was not relevant, because Wendsler had not gone there. Thus, at the trial we watched a long videotape that helped prove that Wendsler had acted lawfully and had no intent to harm the telescope.

The star of the trial was Wendsler. First, he looked magnificent, dressed in a compromise between traditional and modern—a floor-length black vest. I wouldn't be surprised if Wendsler's artist wife Teresa had made it. Many elders of the San Carlos community sat watching silently.

Wendsler Nosie recently, with granddaughter Naelyn Pike. *Photo by Debra Krol.*

With clarity and assurance, Wendsler told the story of his prayer, the thunderstorm and his crashing run down the mountain. The prosecutor's cross examination only increased his credibility. By the final arguments, the prosecutor was focusing not on convicting Wendsler, but on saving the law they had used to prosecute Wendsler from being declared unconstitutional. In the end the Justice of the Peace, Linda Norton, acquitted Wendsler, the only person arrested for "trespassing" on Mount Graham ever to be found not guilty.

165

Mississippi
Set the Course

The sense of human equality that crystallized within me in Mississippi continued throughout my life. No other period or place has had nearly the impact.

I see my "own kind" with a bit more sophistication. I am no longer "white," but people think I am white. So I listen and sometimes tell a story. They think it comes from a white person.

Some things fade with time, like the reaction of caution, born in Mississippi, that through most of my life has accompanied any encounter I have had with a police officer. A very large Black solo beat cop used to walk my childhood neighborhood and knew us all by name. Once again, I can see a policeman as a potential protector, like that officer of my youth, instead of a potential Klan member, like the police in Mississippi.

These days the police seem to ignore my minor transgressions, such as crossing a street where there is no crosswalk. If I were brown and in a conservative suburb, chances are I would be stopped. I would look like the brown-skinned people who have lived in the Southwest for two hundred years or longer. But, as it is, I'm left alone because who would arrest someone for looking only like some illegal Canadian or European?

By luck, I was in Mississippi at a moment to see the possibility, difficulty and excitement of change. I was inspired to continue my education and refine my rudimentary skills so that I could focus my life on using the law to bring about social change. But I also saw that if you simply put yourself where the change is happening, you can be part of it.

America means change. The myth that we are self-made is just that, a myth. We spring from millions of family histories that somehow get molded into an American character, always on the go. Whether that future is dominated by corporate power or individual freedom or something unimagined, I don't know. But as I look back at the stories of some of my ancestors, it seems to me that American freedom and equality have been continuously on the rise, through the efforts of many unknown people. I'm thankful that I was able to choose the direction of my own future.

For me, the key goal of the movement in Mississippi was what I would call American equality. My work had focused on constitutional equality, the kind of equality most readily addressed in the courts: equality of opportunity. All citizens should have a right to vote. There should be no discrimination in governmental programs like schools, courts or public services. Employment opportunities and public accommodations such as restaurants and motels should be equally available to all. Neighborhoods should not exclude particular groups. The criminal justice system should depend on principles of truth, not on privileges of wealth. We should cherish the right to choose and practice one's religion. These are among the core rights of American equality.

On the pediment of the marble temple that houses the United States Supreme Court are the words "Equal Justice Under Law." In essence, what this means is that the *justice system* should treat all equally. It speaks only tangentially to the treatment citizens should receive from legislatures, presidents, governors and agencies. Our founding fathers didn't put economic equality or elimination of poverty in the Constitution. The elimination of starvation and poverty is no less important, but poverty presents problems that are hard to change in court. It's the legislatures that are able to appropriate money and we the people who can contribute in cash or kind.

In 1941, President Franklin Roosevelt recorded the Four Freedoms into the *Congressional Record*:

"...freedom of speech and expression —everywhere in the world.

"...freedom of every person to worship God in his own way—everywhere in the world.

"...freedom from want—which, translated into world terms, means economic understandings which will secure to every nation a healthy peacetime life for its inhabitants—everywhere in the world.

"...freedom from fear—which, translated into world terms, means a world-wide reduction of armaments to such a point and in such a thorough fashion that no nation will be in a position to commit an act of physical aggression against any neighbor—anywhere in the world."

The Courts may be most effective in advancing the first two freedoms. Sometimes chances for reducing poverty and advancing peace are facilitated by establishing freedom of speech and religion. The steady push forward in the courts, in the legislatures, in the foundations and in the streets, seems to me to have resulted in a better world.

Mississippi made me a believer in the best of humanity. I didn't so much learn law there. What I learned was people. I began to see the commonalities of all human beings, while appreciating the varieties of human cultures. As a lawyer, I would need to be able to function effectively for my clients in cultures as diverse as those of Black militants, southern racists and "Black" Cape Verdeans whose culture differed from the general cultures of American Blacks.

The courts can be exciting places. In Mississippi I began to see that the courts are symptoms of society, for better or worse. But since courts are all made up of people, and governed by our constitution, they offer the possibility of the best that human nature can produce. I was starting to learn how to make human contact with those people on the bench and in the jury box. I was beginning to see how law could be a force for social change, not just a bastion of the established power structure.

Law plays a role. But real change occurs at the roots, with local people. My thought as a youth that I could do more as a lawyer is now tempered by the realization that I was always a servant. True leadership more often came from the inspiration of grass roots leaders like Bob Moses, Fannie Lou Hamer, Nate Smith, Al Rojas, Dorothy Crawford, and a neighborhood minister named Martin Luther King, Jr.

The love for people, people unknown, even different in appearance, has remained the blessing of a summer in Mississippi.

Index

Also from ONE MONKEY BOOKS

Hope's Kids: A Voting Rights Summer
by Alan Venable

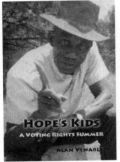

After Selma, spring 1965, Dr. King enlisted Boston area students to go to South Carolina with a Brandeis University SCOPE summer voter registration project. Sheltered in black homes in Richland, Kershaw and Calhoun Counties, South Carolina, they placed themselves in the service of local black leaders in the struggle for civil rights. For these kids, the reward for confronting intimidation, segregation and poverty was a richly rewarding lesson in life.

The Room
by John M. Brewer, Jr.

The memoir of a 1960s Pittsburgh high school rebellion against a legendary "winning" football coach. Some talented players joined the Westinghouse Bulldogs. Others wisely avoided this dominant city-league team. Humorously, compassionately, unflinchingly, Brewer tells how he submitted for glory, battled for truth, and did his part in ending the reign of a damaging coach.

"Fascinating, cover to cover."
  —Midwest Book Review

Ratting on Russo
a novel by Alan Venable

In the East End of Pittsburgh of the late 1950s, outcast, accordion-playing Marty falls under the spell of his eighth-grade classmate, 16-year-old Russo, a lonely, working-class, car-crazy crooner. What could go wrong?

Printed in Great Britain
by Amazon

55714922R10111